LETTERS TO A
STARSEED

LETTERS TO A
STARSEED

Messages and Activations for
Remembering Who You Are
and Why You Came Here

REBECCA CAMPBELL

HAY HOUSE

Carlsbad, California • New York City
London • Sydney • New Delhi

Published in the United Kingdom by:
Hay House UK Ltd, The Sixth Floor, Watson House,
54 Baker Street, London W1U 7BU
Tel: +44 (0)20 3927 7290; Fax: +44 (0)20 3927 7291; www.hayhouse.co.uk

Published in the United States of America by:
Hay House Inc., PO Box 5100, Carlsbad, CA 92018-5100
Tel: (1) 760 431 7695 or (800) 654 5126
Fax: (1) 760 431 6948 or (800) 650 5115; www.hayhouse.com

Published in Australia by:
Hay House Australia Pty. Ltd, 18/36 Ralph St, Alexandria NSW 2015
Tel: (61) 2 9669 4299; Fax: (61) 2 9669 4144; www.hayhouse.com.au

Published in India by:
Hay House Publishers India, Muskaan Complex,
Plot No.3, B-2, Vasant Kunj, New Delhi 110 070
Tel: (91) 11 4176 1620; Fax: (91) 11 4176 1630; www.hayhouse.co.in

A catalogue record for this book is available from the British Library.

Tradepaper ISBN: 978-1-4019-6332-3
E-book ISBN: 978-1-78817-616-3
Audiobook ISBN: 978-1-78817-596-8

Interior images: 1, 95, 145: Shutterstock.com/Subbotina Anna

13 12 11 10 9 8 7 6 5 4

Printed in the United States of America

△
CONTENTS

I REMEMBER
Why Did You Come Here?

PLANT YOURSELF HERE
How to Feel More at Home on Earth

Your soul *had a dream, your* life *is it.*

△
INTRODUCTION

Ever since I was young, I've been deeply fascinated by the big questions of life. Who are we? What is the soul? What are we doing here? According to Plato, devoted student of Socrates, Socrates said that it's the state of our soul, or inner being, which determines the quality of our life.

A mystic at heart, I've chosen to devote my life to living into this great mystery. To reaching for the part of us that existed before we took our first breath and will live on after we exhale our last. And the deeper I get in my exploration of the journey of the soul, the more I'm certain of the mystery itself. Indeed, it's true what they say: The more we know, the less we know.

To me, the Starseed concept is twofold. Firstly, to see yourself as a Starseed is to acknowledge that your soul exists beyond this life and has experienced places beyond this planet. Secondly, to identify as a Starseed is to acknowledge that you're intrinsically connected to all things in nature, the Universe, and beyond.

The Starseed concept is very far from anything I grew up with. However, while the notion that there's an inextinguishable part of us that's experienced places other than Earth did seem quite 'out there' when I first encountered it, it also felt deeply familiar and true to me. It was as if an ancient seed, planted long ago, had been awakened inside me and had started to bud and bloom.

I began learning more deeply about the journey of the soul, and how, just as in this life our experiences influence who we are as a person, our soul's experiences from lifetime to lifetime and all that comes in between influence who we are as a soul.

I was led to train in the intuitive arts and the Akashic Records, where I undertook structured learning to remember the origins of my own soul history and learned processes to support others in doing the same. For five years I was guided to do soul readings for thousands of people all over the world and was given a front seat that allowed me to witness people from all walks of life remembering their ancient soul selves.

In 2015 I began receiving the energy for a book called *Letters to a Starseed*, but the timing wasn't quite right. Looking back now, I can see that if I *had* written that book then, it would have been a very different book to the one you're reading now.

In 2017 I fulfilled a long-term dream to begin sharing the visions I'd had of the journey of the soul by creating the *Work Your Light Oracle* with illustrator Danielle Noel. The following year we created *The Starseed Oracle*, with the intention of activating and transmitting a deep soul remembering in Starseeds to support them in their current incarnation.

Then in 2020, I was invited to write the *Letters to a Starseed* book. I'd just given birth to my son and was in the depths of writing another book focusing on the themes of returning to the Earth, the Mother, and weaving the soul into everyday life, and so logically, it made no sense for me to take on this new project. But when I meditated on it again and again, I got a clear 'yes' to doing so. Like most things in 2020, there seemed to be a different plan destined than the one I'd made.

I was clearly guided that the new book must focus less on looking to the stars and more on supporting Starseeds to commit to their current incarnation here on Earth. On planting ourselves here and remembering the ancient seeds of the soul. *Letters to a Starseed* is the result of that.

In the chapter 'What Is a Starseed?' I explore the different interpretations of the Starseed concept, and my own beliefs about it, in greater depth. I want to be clear that this book isn't an attempt to propose a new theory of evolution or the origins of the human experience; rather, it's focused on the mysterious journey of the soul, how this journey has influenced who we are today, and how we can call all parts of ourselves to truly be here now.

There are many books and much channeled information on the topic of Starseeds from which I've gotten comfort over the years. But I wrote this book to help Starseeds to seed and plant themselves fully here. To embrace their human experience in all of its extremes and get clear on why they're here now.

While I recognize that there are different beliefs about our origins – one of which is that the human body evolved from the salty oceanic depths – I personally believe that there's more to who we are than our physical body and mind. And although this book asks questions like 'Who are we?' and 'Where did we come from?' it does so from the perspective of the soul alone, not the human body. I believe that our souls are eternal, that we choose very consciously to incarnate into physical bodies, and that the soul, the body, and the mind are all equally sacred and holy.

I believe that now more than ever we must commit to being here on Earth. To embody our soul right down into our cells. At this time when the polarity of Earth seems to be at an all-time high and we're unable to look away any longer, we must find a way to be fully here now.

A natural tendency of the sensitive (and many Starseeds identify as highly sensitive) is to disassociate and yearn to be someplace else that feels more like 'home.' However, I do believe that we're being guided to remember why we chose to come and that if we're here, it's because, from a soul perspective, we chose it.

This is a book for those who at times feel misplaced in the world; those who have always felt a remembering of some other place without quite knowing what that place really is.

Throughout these pages, I speak about this longing for home and our potential cosmic ancestry, but I do it as a way of acknowledging the feelings you may have felt at a soul level, so you can commit to being even more present in your current life, here and now today.

It's important that we don't spend our days here longing to be someplace else. This book isn't designed to help you lose yourself in the stars, but rather to support you so that you can be more present to your life, to humanity, and to the planet.

We are living in urgent times. And I believe that, due to the unconscious ways we've been living and the unsustainable harm we've been causing the planet, we're also living in a time of mass-awakening and spiritual integration. It's clear that something needs to shift if the Earth is to be a place that humanity can continue to call home. I believe that we're being urged to remember who we are, our place in the Universe as a whole, and the part we're being called to play in this great metamorphosis on planet Earth.

I've been blessed with incredible teachers who've taught me to trust the voice of my soul above all else. My intention in this book, and in all of my work, is to support you in listening to that part of *you* above all else. I can only ever speak from my own experience, and in offering up what I discover along the way, my ponderings, and my story, my aim is to support you on your unique journey. If something I say resonates with you and supports you, that's great. If something I share doesn't align with you, then always stay true to you.

I'm writing this book as someone who has deep faith but doesn't align to one particular religion or tradition alone. I have great respect for all traditions, practices, and paths, and the human right to choose. If I use a word or phrase that's not the same as those you use, please feel into the energy and devotional intent behind it and replace it with your own word or phrase. All paths, faiths, belief systems, traditions, and people are welcome here, and I hope you feel that in these pages.

Throughout the book you'll find such terms as 'Universe,' 'pulse of life,' 'the Great Mother,' 'the great mystery,' 'Life,' and 'Source,' all of which refer to the intelligence that transcends all religions and all things.

You'll also find terms such as 'soul' and 'ancient self.' Here, I'm referring to the part of you that's inextinguishable and eternal; the part that exists beyond this life and that you carry from lifetime to lifetime; the part that may have experienced places far beyond this one; the part that's connected to the intelligent pulse of the entire Universe; and the part that's waiting to guide you, every moment of every day.

Another word that I use is 'cosmos' or 'cosmic.' *The Collins English Dictionary* defines cosmic as 'belonging or relating to the Universe.' While Earth itself is of course part of the Universe, I believe that some souls have experienced far more than just this life on this planet, and that through inquiring into the mystery of our own soul we can begin to catch a small glimpse of the part we play in the great cosmos of Life.

As with many of my creations, this book has consciously been written in short chapters to allow you to easily read and digest it at your own pace. Think of each chapter as like a letter or a mini conversation. You can read the chapters one at a time or all in one sitting. You can also use the book as an oracle – first, pray to whatever force you believe in and then open a page at random for the possibility of being met where you are.

These pages are devoted to helping you to trust that inner system. As you read them, if anything I've written doesn't meet you where you're at, then just take what does. My work is always intended to support people on their inner journey, as each of us is equipped with a guidance system that's far more powerful than anything outside of ourselves.

Throughout the book you'll find two prompts, which will support you on your journey as you read:

- **Soul Inquiry®** I'm a big believer in the power of listening to the whispers of your soul and then acting on them. In many chapters, you'll find Soul Inquiry prompts that will help you hear the calls of your soul as you journey through the book. When answering, try not to overthink it; instead trust what comes without it having to make sense. Feel free to jot down your answers in a special notebook, or you can even write them directly into the book.

- **Starseed Activation** In some chapters, you'll also find activations. These are here to support you in activating and integrating energies and healing within you, from your soul to your cells. Whenever possible, I recommend saying these activations out loud (even if it's a whisper), and for extra power, repeat them three times.

There are also meditations, attunements, and Soul Journeys featured and mentioned throughout, which you can find on the book's website: www.letterstoastarseed.com. If you'd like to enhance your listening experience I've shared on that same website the Letters to a Starseed Spotify playlist to which I wrote the book. If you feel inspired to share on social media while you read, you can find me @rebeccacampbell_ author and the book hashtag is #LetterstoaStarseed.

My hope for this book is that it supports, comforts, and inspires you to remember who you truly are and why you chose to be here at this pivotal moment in the story of humanity. To commit fully to being here and being present to your life on Earth at this time. To encourage you to play the note that you came here to play, without waver.

The awakening process is one of remembering, and right now, we're all waking up and remembering at a rapid rate. Consciousness seems to be shifting each and every day. As a planet, we're waking up to the reality that the ancient prophecies and warnings of the elders and wise ones are no longer predictions but our reality. They're not just coming or even near – we're actually living them right now.

It's becoming alarmingly clear that what we do now matters to the future of this planet. We can no longer push the reality of our global situation under the rug and pretend it's not happening.

We're living in a time between myths and stories. I believe that we're currently reweaving the fabric of life on planet Earth. Make no mistake – these are urgent times. And we all have a role to play. Do you remember why you've come?

Love,

EARTHED

Who Are We and Where Did We Come From?

△

The Moment of Your Birth

Before you were born your soul consulted with the
cosmos to arrange the details of your return.

The location and conditions were carefully orchestrated
and seeded as you crossed the threshold of the in-between
– the watery world of the Mother. There you waited in
the fertile void as all of the stars and the planets in the
knowable and unknowable cosmos moved into place.

When the alignment was just right, a portal opened and
you were crowned upon your entrance to the world. A soul
embodied. Spirit planted. Eternal woven into matter.
Heaven and Earth combined.

Your cells, your flesh, your bones, your eyes, all made up of
ancient exploding stars. The Universe magnificently ordered as
the cosmos. Your basic existence is enough to blow anyone's mind.

How did you get here? And why did you choose to come?
Somehow, the cosmic curtains parted for the
great dance of your life to begin.

This is that life and you are that dancer.
It took a lot for you to be here now.
To be planted here now.
And what a time you chose to come.

△
WHAT IS A STARSEED?

For as long as I can remember, I've been deeply involved with the meaning of life, the exploration of consciousness, our place in the Universe, and in particular, the eternal part of us that I call the soul.

What is the soul? How does it influence who we are? Why did we choose to incarnate? Where does the soul go when we die? These questions, and many others like them, continue to fascinate and consume me.

It was through living questions such as these that in 2010 I came across a word that would have a significant impact on my life – bigger than any other prior or since. It was as if it had always been waiting for me to find it. I was forever changed. That word was 'Starseed.'

As I learned more about the concept of 'Starseed,' something seemed to come alive within me. I felt both excitement and a deep sense of calm, as I was able to put a name to something I'd always felt but had lacked the words to explain. It helped me to be more present to my life and to the unfolding mystery.

The first known reference to the word Starseed was made by the US psychologist Dr. Timothy Leary, who used it to describe a drawing of the remnant of a living organism (an extraterrestrial) found on a meteorite on Earth. But the word means a lot more than life other than on Earth. Most commonly, it's used to describe souls who have experienced 'something and someplace' other than life on this planet. Souls who have not only incarnated on Earth but have also had experiences in other places.

I resonate with this interpretation of the word Starseed and I'm still feeling into the deep mystery and questions within it. Perhaps only some souls are Starseeds. Or maybe all souls are, with some of us recognizing ourselves more clearly in this concept because the veil of remembering is thinner, or because an 'activation' (a switching on, a remembering, or an awakening at mind, body, and soul level) has occurred.

Or perhaps some souls have spent more time (or more recent times) incarnating in places other than Earth and this is why it's easier for them to remember the interconnectedness of Life and to feel certain that we're not alone in this Universe. Either way, I believe that a Starseed is someone who understands the infinite capacities of consciousness.

> **Starseeds know that they're part of something bigger than them and that everything is interconnected. They've woken up to the fact that we're not the center of the Universe, that Life exists beyond our limited idea of it, and that we're connected to all of Life, both on this planet and in the entire Universe.**

A Starseed is someone who knows that they are a multidimensional being and that there is more to Life than we see here on Earth. A multidimensional being is someone who knows that they are made up of more than just mind and body. Some people come in with this knowing, the seed of remembering within them already active. Others awaken to it.

I believe that many Starseeds have heard the call to play their part in the great dance of Life and have chosen to be here at this time in history. The seed within them has been activated.

Perhaps being a Starseed is more about having had the consciousness within us awakened and activated in this way than it is about who we are at an innate soul level. Perhaps some souls come in with that innate memory, that remembering, while others wake up to it at some point in their lives, and others remain asleep.

The journey and origins of the soul is probably the greatest philosophical mystery known to humankind. It's a topic that's captivated philosophers, mystics, scientists, poets, and artists throughout the ages.

And while right now it's impossible to attach certainty to any of the great mysteries, especially this one, what I do know is that from a young age I've had memories and experienced glimpses of something other than the life I'm currently living. I've experienced spontaneous rememberings of lives and experiences other than this one, and had visions of places other than Earth. I've tried to portray many of these visions in my oracle decks. Through my work over the years I've discovered that I'm not alone in this. Perhaps you too have had flashes of these rememberings? I believe that these rememberings come from the imprinted memories of the soul.

A Starseed knows their place in the Universe and sees this life as but a moment in their soul's journey. They recognize that they're an ever-changing, eternal being and part of a great cosmic dance. They understand that they're connected to the plants and the stones, just as they're connected to the Sun, the stars, the planets, and the Moon.

They're awake to the fact that life is ever-changing and that they're a soul having a human experience. They recognize that they're not special and also extremely special – just like all of Life. That they, like all beings, have a unique note to play and that there's a reason why they chose to come.

Some believe that Starseeds currently make up only a small fraction of the population here on Earth and are beginning to incarnate in increasing numbers. Some believe that many Starseeds have been incarnating over and over again to prepare us for this time. Perhaps this is true of all of us. It's my belief that a Starseed is a soul who actively chose to be here now, at this pivotal moment in history, to influence the outcome of the time in which we're living. And what a time this is.

My whole life, I've felt this urgency, this call, this faint pressure from deep within, to remember why I came. Maybe you have too. As a young girl I'd tell my mum that there was something I came here to do, and that I wasn't the only one. The journey from then to writing these words in these pages has been a rocky, and at times extremely lonely, one. The urgency would keep me up on many a night and it drove me to work as hard as I could to find my soul's path – something I didn't have the words for but always felt calling me toward it.

I believe that many Starseeds come into this life with a seed or a spark that's forever calling them to remember why they have come. Perhaps it's this very seed or spark that called them here in the first place.

Perhaps this seed, this spark, exists within each of us. Dormant in some, activated and active in others.

I believe that Starseeds are intelligently placed all over the planet and that when awoken, activated, and integrated, their presence has an energetic impact on the world. I believe that many have been training and preparing for this period of history for many lifetimes. I believe that each soul has a unique note to play in the great re-orchestration – and that the re-orchestration is happening now.

I woke up to the first seeds of my soul's calling relatively young; however, it took me almost two decades to gather the courage to trust, surrender to, and act on this call in a grounded, practical way. And, as is the case for most people, my journey has been anything but straightforward.

In my late teens I began working several part-time jobs so that I could afford to train in the intuitive, mystic arts and read as much as possible about the journey of the soul and our place in the Universe. I didn't see this natural fascination and passion as a legitimate path, but as something that I kept in my personal life. In my twenties I began stepping out of the spiritual closet by offering sessions in my spare time from my job as a conceptual creative and creative director.

Before long, it became very clear from the people who showed up for these sessions that I was here to support souls who remembered that they'd come here for a reason – souls who had both an *individual* soul mission (here for their own soul's growth) and a *collective* soul mission (here to influence something in the collective together with others). I began to call this 'having a double mission.' (We'll explore this more in the chapter 'Soul Mission.')

As the years passed and I worked with thousands of people all over the world, I began to see a resemblance between people who, although outwardly extremely diverse and from every walk of life, shared similar traits from a soul perspective. I noticed that many had a clear knowing from a very young age that there was something they'd come here to do, and that they felt like time was running out for them to do it.

This knowing seemed to be innate, rather than learned. Many of these people felt isolated or alone in the part of the world in which they'd been planted, and as if they were 'the weird one' in their family, school, suburb, or town; they longed deeply for like-souled people to connect with. I so related. The further my work reached and the more people I began working with, the more patterns I began to see emerge. I had a clear vision of these souls being carefully placed and planted in the soil of the world, as if the location, details, and timing of their birth and upbringing were carefully orchestrated.

Some were born into families who were very different to them from a soul perspective, while others had upbringings that would support their journey more quickly. Each soul with their own personal syllabus, but working together on collective soul missions – some here to break down archaic systems and structures; some here to clear things ancestrally; some here to birth things anew; some here for karmic reasons; some here to support and midwife; some here to ignite and activate; some here to clear the way for the new souls that are coming.

I noticed that once they're awake, most Starseeds find it extremely hard to have meaningless conversations, jobs, and relationships. They innately know that there's much more to life and get to work in living that. They can find the pace of the world, and how slow people and systems are to change, frustrating.

I discovered that many who resonate with being a Starseed had significant 'awakening' experiences from a relatively young age. Many Starseeds confess to feeling extremely different – as if they don't fit into the world – and they long for a place or people to support them in feeling more 'at home.'

I'd like to add here that, particularly in the West, we've become so disconnected from the land and our own ancestors that this feeling of displacement can also be heightened in a physical way and it requires deep work to address it. I acknowledge that having access to the resources to do so is a great privilege.

On some level many Starseeds remember the unity that is possible, so they tend to want to check out from the world (transcend it) because of the deep pain that comes with separation. If you resonate with this, I urge you to commit to being here now. I know that at times, the polarity here on Earth – the opposite and sometimes contradictory experiences that come with being human – can feel too much to bear. I know that from a soul perspective you may long for the oneness of Source or spirit. However, these are changing times. Earth is a planet of polarity and if you're here it's because your soul chose to be here in a body now.

When we check out and focus solely on oneness (ignoring the current reality of the Earth experience), it has an impact on the planet energetically. When we check out or bypass the difficult or the uncomfortable, we're avoiding the reality of the human experience. If you have a tendency to do this, you're not alone. And now is the time for us to really dig deep. To commit to being here with every cell of our bodies. To call all parts of our soul to return – all the way in.

Because some Starseeds feel so 'different' it's not uncommon for them to spend part of their lives trying to fit in, or being in some form of spiritual or other 'closet.' However, fitting ourselves into a box goes against who we are from a soul perspective. Multifaceted. Exquisitely unique. The more we do this, the more isolated, unseen, and alone we'll likely feel. The more we embrace our uniqueness and courageously show the world who we are, the easier it is for our people to find us and for us to create a life that feels as if it's in alignment with who we are from a soul perspective. The more we hide ourselves, the more alone and not at home we'll feel, both in ourselves and in the world.

With Scorpio as my rising sign, I've always felt comfortable in the depths and willing to dive deep into the shadows in order to alchemize. Looking back now I see that I used to live in a way where the spiritual life and the human life existed simultaneously but still somehow felt separate. I see now how this separation has caused so many problems in the world and stops true healing or unity from happening. I believe that we're now beginning to address this severing and that there's an ancient call for true integration to happen.

This time in which we're living is urging us to stay present to all that's happening. To hold the opposite poles of the human experience in order to bring about lasting unity and to genuinely weave the soul, the cosmic, the sacred, and the Divine into the Earth, into matter, and into our physical, everyday human lives.

△

ANCIENT STARS IN OUR BONES

Scientists have been saying for some time that we're made of stardust. It's not a poetic statement, it's a fact – we're deeply connected to the Universe at a cellular level. Your body – right down to your organs, your cells, and your bones – is made of ancient exploded stars.

Stardust is continually moving through us, rebuilding our bodies again and again and again with every breath and every moment. I wonder, are we all made up of the same ancient stars? Or are we each a combination of different ones? Re-constellating ourselves as we spin our way around the world in our minute corner of the Universe?

Do those ancient stars echo on in our bones? Is that what we can see in the unique, intricate, breathtaking beauty that is the irises of our eyes? Or is the soul the creator of that masterpiece? A unique fingerprint. A new spec created with each new lesson, loss, initiation, dark night, gift, and life?

And where did the soul originate? Why don't we all remember? What is it that we forget? Will we ever really know?

All parts of this planet are made up of the same star stuff. As Karel and Iris Schrijver explain in their book *Living with the Stars*: 'Our bodies are made of the burned-out embers of stars that were released into the galaxy in massive explosions long before gravity pulled them to form the Earth. Those remnants now comprise essentially all the materials in our bodies.'[1]

This is true not only of us but of every object, every organism, every single living thing.

Perhaps that's why all of the Universe's secrets can be found by looking into a lover's eyes. Or at a flower. Or a tree. Or a single wave. Supernovas. Luminous stellar explosions. As above, so below.

Planet Earth is indeed cosmic – it's easy to forget that. We're but a speck of dust, a single seed in the Universe. And that's just the one we know. Will we remember before it's too late that we're not the very center of the Universe? That it's inconceivable that we're the only ones out there, here? Will we wake up to the fact that we're all more alike than we are different? Bone, flesh, heartbeat. Ancient souls in human bodies. Diverse and different, and also made up of the very same things.

△

REACHING BACK TO
THE ANCIENTS

Mystics, theologians, philosophers, scientists, visionaries, saints, poets, and wise elders through the ages have grappled with the difficulty of explaining the mystery of the stars and our place in the Universe. The part of us that exists beyond our physical world on Earth. The intelligent life force that's breathing us. The pulse that causes the planets to spin and the seasons to come and go.

The part of us that remembers and is eternal – which comes in knowing and survives the certainty of the death of the physical body; the intelligent part of us that's connected to the mysterious intelligence of the Universe.

The ancients looked to the night sky to understand who they were and their place and purpose in the Universe. This can be seen in the many myths and stories from all corners of the world that were passed down by word of mouth in ancient lost languages – the mystery of creation and our connection to the stars echoes on and on. It's believed that ancient communities relied on the oral transmission of these myths and stories by shepherds, storytellers, wise ones, medicine people, priests and priestesses, and farmers.

Through observing the star-filled canopy above, the ancients saw that the Sun, the Moon, and the stars followed certain paths through the skies that corresponded with the seasons, while the planets followed a different rhythm. For example, the ancient Egyptians noticed that the annual rising of Sirius (the brightest star in the night sky, also called Alpha Canis Majoris or the Dog Star) coincided with the season of flooding of the River Nile, an event that's still acknowledged to this day.

According to the Australian scholar Ragbir Bhathal, long before European civilizations had named the observable planets and stars in the night sky, the 'indigenous people of Australia had not only given them names but had also built an astronomical knowledge system which they incorporated into their social, cultural and religious life.'[1]

The indigenous people of Australia have been sharing their Dreaming stories of the sky for at least 40,000 years. For example, many groups use the orientation of the constellation known as the great celestial emu to determine the best time to collect emu eggs. When the great celestial emu is on the eastern horizon after sunset, it signals that the Earthly emus are nesting – which means there are no emu eggs available. Later in the year, the emu constellation is higher in the sky, and once its body is overhead after sunset, it's time to collect emu eggs.

Some of the world's creation
stories are linked to the stars.

Ancient Egyptian texts suggest that the gods themselves came from the stars – Osiris from the major constellation Orion, Isis from Sirius, and so on – and together they created humanity. The Pyramids of Giza in Egypt, one of the Seven Wonders of the World, were built in precise alignment with the three stars in Orion's Belt (Mintaka, Alnitak, and Alnilam).

On the other side of the planet, the pyramids of the Sun, the Moon, and Quetzalcoatl in the ancient Mesoamerican city of Teotihuacan, near modern-day Mexico City, also line up with Orion in perfect precision, and myths say that the gods came to Earth in this exact place of cosmic alignment. And in Mexico's Yucatan Peninsula, the ancient Maya built stone temples and observatories so they could watch the stars above them; they're also renowned for the incredible precision of their astronomical calendar.

In Mali in West Africa, the Dogon tribe has an incredible legend and ceremony centered on Sirius. The ceremony, called the Sigui, takes place when Sirius hits a particular landmark in the night sky and is based on the legend that some 3,000 years ago amphibious beings from Sirius visited the tribe.

In Wiltshire, UK, the Neolithic Avebury henge and stone circle was created in alignment with the Milky Way; and the standing stone circle at nearby Stonehenge was carefully aligned to receive the first rays of sun on the summer and winter solstices. Worldwide, there are more temples and other places of worship that indicate similar incredible star alignment. In fact, countless stone circles and temples were built in alignment with the summer and winter solstices in ancient times, including the temple complex at Karnak in Egypt and Buena Vista in Peru, to name two.

The importance of the stars and sky is revealed in myth and legend too. Celtic starlore whispers of fairies falling to Earth, while Greek mythology speaks of the creation of star systems such as Taurus 'the Bull,' and references the Hyades and the Pleiades, two open star clusters that were noted by many ancient civilizations.

Orion, in Greek mythology, was a hunter associated with the constellation now known by his name, and in Celtic tradition too, Orion was associated with hunting – with the phantom hunter Herne, the god Cernunnos, the mythological king Gwyn ap Nudd, and Aran.

Pegasus, a constellation in the northern sky, has had a rich and varied meaning across civilizations. In Greek legend it was identified with the winged horse Pegasus, which could use its hooves to dig water springs that would provide poetic flow to writers in search of inspiration; the constellation was later named after the mythical horse. The Celts spoke of the same constellation as 'the horse of Llyr,' the sea god – a beautiful white beast that appeared in many Celtic myths. Today, we still refer to the whitecaps of waves on the sea as 'white horses.'

In Arizona, USA, the Native American Anasazi culture (ancestors of the Hopi people) built settlements on three mesas (flat-topped hills) that were aligned with the shape of Orion. And the creation myths of the Native American Cherokee, Onondaga, Pawnee, and Seneca peoples speak of the 'Star Woman.'[2] Within these stories is the possibility of direct physical relations between Earth and sky people.

In Pawnee mythology the Sun, the Moon, and the stars are worshipped as gods – the Evening Star (feminine) and the Morning Star (masculine) came together to create the first humans. The Pawnee also worked with the wisdom of the stars when planting their corn crops, to ensure bountiful harvests.[3]

Where does the soul originate? How did we end up here? Where do we go when we die? These are some of the greatest questions of all time. When we look at ancient archeoastronomy, we can't help but wonder – did the ancients know more about our origins than we do? What did they know about our connection with the stars? And will these mysteries be revealed in our lifetime?

△
HERE WE ARE

Some believe that Starseeds are souls who answered a call to be here at this pivotal time in history. There's no denying that right now, as a planet, we're navigating a global dark night crisis and a possible invitation for the evolution of a whole new humanity.

At times, it can feel like we're living in a pressure cooker. A death of our old ways is happening, that's for sure, and it's becoming clear that rebirth isn't possible without consciously living through the contractions and letting them change us. We must let them change us as a species.

Many of us have already been through our own personal awakenings in the few decades leading up to this moment. You could say that in a way, we've been preparing for this for years, perhaps even lifetimes.

However, the majority of people are being startled from their slumber to find themselves right in the middle of the birth canal – somewhere between death and a possible planetary rebirth. The awakening process isn't easy at the best of times, and right now, with the world the way it is, with all of the polarization and all of the harm humanity has done, it's not easy to wake up.

Regardless of which stage of our awakening journey we find ourselves in (the awakening process never ends), we're all waking up to the reality that the ancient philosophies and warnings from the elders are no longer predictions but our current reality. We're living in them right now. What we do now matters. We can't push the reality of our global situation under the rug and pretend it's not happening. Whether we like it or not, we're going through this death and possible rebirth together.

It's clear that living unconsciously – and in a way where we separate ourselves from nature and each other – is no longer a sustainable option. The Mother herself is urging us urgently to heed her call before it's too late (for us, not for her). And she's been calling for some time. But it's becoming clear that in order for us to return to her arms and navigate our way through this tumultuous time in human history, we must find a way to come together and mend what's been severed. We must remember who we are, why we came, and commit to truly being here.

I believe that all souls who are here on the Earth right now chose on some level to be here. I also believe that some of those souls came here as a kind of birthing team – a group of souls who chose to take on the challenge of these times. To support humanity in remembering who we are. To support us in coming back home to each other and planet Earth. To truly return to love. And it's important to realize that love isn't possible without being with what is. Just as oneness isn't possible without acknowledging the severing that's occurred over and over again.

In many ways this is a very painful time to be alive; and from a soul perspective it can be seen as an incredible one too because of how much rapid change is taking place. I believe that at a soul level you chose to be here right now, for this. To be part of this, and to influence the outcome of this.

I believe that you being here – in this body that you find yourself in, in the city that you find yourself in, in this time that you find yourself in – is no random fluke, and from a soul perspective, we chose this. And I believe that you being here, we being here, matters. Now that we're awake, may we play our part and take consistent grounded action on the calls of our soul in order to return again and again and again.

Returning

We are Children of the Earth and the Sky.
Eternal souls having a human experience.

This   but   stitch   the   of
*   life   a   in   tapestry   humanity.*

Humanity but a turn in the spinning of the Earth.
Held on this planet by gravity, breath, and time.

Falling

falling

falling

for the exquisite, agonizing glory of
experiencing ourselves and each other.

Finding home where we find ourselves.

Not quite able to remember, or to forget,
our other homes in the sky.

△
THE LONGING FOR HOME

Hiraeth is a Welsh word that's difficult to translate into English but it refers to a certain longing or homesickness. A nostalgia or yearning for a home or a place to which we cannot return. This unexplainable, unshakable longing for 'home,' without even knowing what that means, is common in Starseeds.

For some, it's a distant memory of a place that their soul remembers and yearns to return to. Somewhere or sometime they may have experienced prior to the here and now. For others, it's a longing for the unity of Source. A remembering of interconnected oneness that's so polar to the separation felt by so many of us right now on Earth.

I believe that it's possible to create this feeling of 'home' on Earth and that the concept of creating heaven on Earth is what this is about. To seed the soul into the cells. Many of us get a glimpse of this 'at home' feeling when we meditate or spend time in nature, only to be abruptly pulled out of it, and we spend our lives dancing between the two. In many ways our disconnection from nature makes this yearning more distinct. Both our soul and our body faintly remembering the potential of true interconnection.

I think that for many of us, the original severing – the first one that we experience – can occur right after our mothers have given birth. We go from being in the warm waters of the womb, where all of our needs are met, to, in many cases, a brightly lit room where we're suddenly separate from our mother, our previous home.

I believe that prior to being in the womb our soul chose to come here and it did so from a place much different from here. I believe that the soul chose to re-experience itself through the human experience, which is a great adventure in itself; and that the soul is more used to being in places where separation doesn't exist as it does here.

The more time the soul has spent in these places, the deeper the separation that can be felt and the more distinct the longing can be.

This yearning can lead some to travel and roam, searching all corners of the planet to find a physical place that feels more like 'home.'

For others it can manifest as a need to find 'home' in people. A journey to find somewhere they truly belong or someone they truly belong to. As a species, so many of us are so separate from each other, particularly in the West. We see ourselves as the center, or rather the top, of life on Earth itself, bending and controlling everything to our will. It's this patriarchal striving to be on top and conquer that makes us feel more and more alone, disconnected, and misplaced.

If you resonate with feeling misplaced or have this yearning for home but don't really know where home is or even really what it means, it's helpful to remember that your soul chose to be here in this body on Earth at this time. I believe that the memory of the 'at homeness' that Starseeds feel can result in us wanting to escape the pain and separation that's so apparent in the world right now. And while it makes perfect sense for us to yearn and long for this, it's becoming more and more obvious that it's not going to become a reality until we all do our part, and until every one of us is protected, equal, cherished, and free.

The longing for home can be magnified when you consider our own ancestral history. Many of us are living on land that's different from that of our ancestors, whether through the globalization of travel or the many brutal outcomes of colonialism, amongst other things. Perhaps Starseeds have a tendency toward transcendence because of their experiences of places other than here; perhaps this is the reason many Starseeds find it difficult to fathom why humanity continues to separate itself in groups and otherness. Why it builds walls and borders; why it divides and conquers. Perhaps these are the very structures, systems, and ways of being that we came here to dismantle. And that true unity can only take place when we fully integrate the sacred here on Earth.

It's becoming clear that these times we're in are about just that – unlearning, unwinding, dismantling, and rebuilding. In order to find our way back to each other and to truly feel at home here and with each other we need to allow this dismantling and rebuilding to happen. And, if it eases the longing just a bit, to look at this life as a great adventure for your soul and call any part of you that's checked out to come fully back in.

STARSEED ACTIVATION

'I choose to plant myself here and commit to my incarnation.

I choose to see this life as a great adventure for the soul.

I choose to actively create home where I am now.

I choose to call all parts of me fully back in.'

△
WHAT A TIME TO COME

With the arrival of 2020, I began receiving inner guidance that many Starseeds were completing collective soul missions and some were beginning new ones. As if it were some sort of transition point when it came to collective soul missions.

The human part of us needs time to recover, and the soul is being directed to come more fully into the body. The more time we've spent in the higher chakras, the deeper we need to plant ourselves into the Earth right now.

The deeper we enter into our incarnation, the more of an impact we can have and the further our light can travel. It's time now to truly embody what we've learned spiritually, and it's also a time of undoing.

As many collective soul missions are ending and beginning again it can feel like a double death. Discombobulating. It's meant to. We're all renegotiating and recommitting.

If you're questioning everything you ever knew to be true, good. This is what it is to die and be born anew.

Many souls are experiencing a lot of grief right now as the entire world wakes up collectively. No matter how blissful your awakening, waking up isn't pretty. And this is happening each and every day. It's a lot. And it needs to be. We're waking up to who we are; we're waking up to the fact that our planet may not be able to survive with us on it, and that the extinction of the human species (as well as millions of others) is a possible outcome. And most tragically, to the realization that the way we've been treating the world, its beings, and each other has caused it all.

This isn't your fault alone, and it's not yours alone to carry. But together, those of us standing here now on this planet must step forward and take responsibility for where we are as a species. We must let these times initiate us into taking consistent, grounded, genuine action.

We're each the child of someone. We learned our ways from those who did incredible things, those who didn't know any better, and those who did know better but decided to overlook it. We must now acknowledge where we are and how we got here.

Now is the time to shift gears, to open our minds and our hearts to each other. To open ourselves up to solutions that are different from anything that's been thought of before. To fully commit to this planet and each other and seed the soul deeply into the Earth. No more escaping to the heavens to avoid the density – we must be in this polar ship together. And no matter how divided and separated we are, at the end of the day we really are in this together.

For too long so many of us who are 'awake' have disassociated ourselves from humanity. This could have happened as part of the awakening process or some kind of trauma. The understanding of trauma has come a long way, and there are many therapies that can support its treatment. I also acknowledge that having access to therapy is a privilege. Sometimes our difficult experiences cause us on some level to decide that the world is too harsh, too dense, for us; too painful to be here fully. But this has the potential to be a new day, the beginning of a new era – even, as some are saying, the potential for a new world. We have the opportunity to be the birthers of whatever it is that's possible.

There will be contractions. Labor, just like the awakening process, isn't smooth and easy. We're healing and clearing, processing and grieving, awakening and shifting, just as we should. No one is immune to this human experience.

For some of us, the original wound can be as early as the moment of our birth. Arriving Earth-side and realizing we've arrived somewhere that's not 'home,' that's not Source. The separation of soul and body occurs.

I believe that one of the goals of this time is to find a way to plant heaven onto the Earth, or rather, recognize it here. To weave the sacred back here. As above, so below. To remember the ancient ways and birth new ones too, or to remember where our soul is not recognized or received. If we're going to stand a chance of doing so we must face all of the ways we've separated ourselves from the Earth and each other. We're all children of history and while our soul may have been part of creating history, we also know that the state of the world can't be the fault of any one person alone.

If we're here now it's because on some level our soul chose to be here now. It's very clear that the way we've been living, and the harm we've been inflicting, has to stop. Or *we'll* be stopped once and for all. This is the greatest, most unfathomable healing of all. Until we do this, true oneness will never be possible. Together we're creating the consciousness that will determine the future of the world.

It's normal to feel that what's happening is personal, because no person is immune to what's happening in the world in this time. And no person is alone in what's happening in the world in this time.

May we remember our true nature (we *are* nature), and may we gain enough perspective to find a way from separation to planetary unity. This doesn't mean that the human experience will be all roses – quite the contrary.

This is a planet of poles, of opposites, of extremes. Being a human is extreme at the best of times. And we happen to be living in times that are very extreme.

The polarity of this planet is real. The density of this planet is real. And we can't experience the bliss and the love, the oneness, without experiencing the polar. This is the human experience. We must embrace this. We must remember this. Now more than ever, it's time that we commit to our human experience. Even if we're hurting; especially if we're hurting. As a species, we're experiencing a collective death and initiation. Alchemy is possible. And you're here as an alchemist.

Alchemy isn't all light and love, though – quite the contrary. It requires that we dive deep into the unfathomable depths of the human experience in order to transmute it into gold. Indeed, it's only through the darkness, through surrendering to the darkest of caves to the mystery itself, that true, unshakable, lasting, sustainable light and change is even possible.

STARSEED ACTIVATION

'I surrender to my role as a cosmic alchemist.

I choose to embrace the extremes of my humanity as a path to genuine, sustainable oneness.

I'm committed to seeding my soul into the Earth and coming home to my body.'

△
WHO ARE YOU REALLY?

I've come to believe that we each come in with our own essence and that essence is the soul. This essence is what we see in a newborn child, before the external world has had a chance to imprint anything on it. We're captivated by it, for the potent, innocent, Divine presence invites our own soul forth to witness a similar grace to it and who we are beneath it all.

Remembering who we are as a soul has been some of the most influential work I've done, both personally and professionally. I believe that when we acknowledge the soul we call in more of our life force, for I believe that the soul is itself Life force.

Our soul's unique essence is crafted through all of the experiences it's ever had. Like a multifaceted crystal or a fingerprint, each experience creates a new facet, or a brand new loop, arch, or whorl. As the soul continues its journey, it keeps creating and carrying with it all of these imprints of all of its experiences, from lifetime to lifetime and everything in between.

Who we are at a soul level comes in with us when we're born. It transcends our family of origin and can be sensed by those who know how to see the soul from the moment we take our first breath. In our society we're starved of people who have hearts that can see the soul. Indeed, all souls have this yearning to be seen. Recognized. A deep, ancient longing to be properly greeted when they arrive Earth-side. To be greeted in a way that tells them that after such an epic journey, it is recognized that they have come.

In the next chapter you'll find a long list of soul qualities, gifts, and traits that you might like to use to begin feeling into the multifaceted nature of who you are from a soul perspective. These are the unique qualities of the part of you that existed before you even drew your first breath and which will continue on after you take your last.

Of course, it isn't just our soul that has qualities and traits – these things evolve as we do in our life. Often, our soul traits and gifts can be the ones that don't make perfect sense in terms of our human life or the family or conditions we were born into. One certain way of knowing that these are your soul traits and gifts is that there's no other explanation for them. I've come to realize that from a soul perspective, being different is the whole point. Being different is a clear indication that treasure is there.

While I was growing up, my soul traits and gifts didn't make sense to me, as they were very different from those of the family I was born into. Qualities such as wisdom, mystic, deep-sea diver, and healer didn't make sense to me as a young girl, yet they would lead me into dusty bookshops and working three part-time jobs in the school holidays so I could afford to learn more about them.

When I was young these unshakable qualities made me feel different and weird when I most wanted to fit in. Now I see them as the keys to who I came here to be and what I came here to spend my time doing.

Your soul qualities and gifts can be unexplainable (i.e. different from your upbringing and life conditions) or they can be encouraged or enhanced by your upbringing and life conditions. The qualities that have emerged for me that are true at a soul level are determined, hardworking, focused, and strong-willed. Having worked with the Akashic Records and my past lives throughout my twenties I was able to excavate these. They're also qualities that I share with some of my maternal ancestors, such as my mother, her father, her grandfather, and so on.

So often our soul qualities and gifts are misunderstood while we're growing up. However, in adulthood we can begin to name them, claim them, and create a life that's in alignment with them. The more we name who we are, the easier it is to claim it. The more we claim who we are, the easier it is to embody it each and every day. The more we embody it each and every day, the more in alignment with Life we become.

If you're a parent or have children in your life, one of the greatest gifts you can give a child is to truly see the soul that has come. To thank them for joining you here on Earth. If you're blessed to hold a baby, take a moment to truly witness the soul that has arrived. Life is a great initiation for the soul – it goes through a great journey to arrive here Earth-side. The more you acknowledge it the more likely it'll stay present and anchor itself here through this witnessing. And bring forth the unique qualities that it came here to seed.

And, as you look in the mirror every day, you can do that for you too.

STARSEED ACTIVATION

Look in the mirror, soften your gaze, and lose yourself in the intricate detail of the irises of your eyes. Connect with your soul, your ancient self, the part of you that chose to be here now, and say:

'Thank you for being here. I call all of who I am and all of who I came here to be to Earth now.'

△
MEET YOUR SOUL

We have two parts to us – the human self and the soul self. The human self consists of our mind and body; it's the 'suit' that our soul embodies and uses while we're incarnated on the Earth. The matter in which our soul exists.

I believe that before we're born, our soul consciously chooses the body (which includes within it ancestral patterns, family dynamics, location, and DNA) for our soul's growth, karmic history, and personal and collective soul missions. Without the human self, the soul can't experience itself. Without the soul, the human self ceases to exist. The two are held together with our breath.

The soul is our inextinguishable, eternal self – the part of us that we carry from lifetime to lifetime and beyond. Everything your soul has experienced adds to who you are as a soul. I believe that as souls we've experienced many lifetimes here on Earth and that many of us have been influenced by experiences in places in the vast cosmos beyond this planet.

The soul carries karmic impressions, which are imprinted memories, gifts, vows, contracts, and experiences. There's a Sanskrit word that forms the basis for this karmic theory: *samskara*. *Samskaras* are mental impressions, rememberings, or psychological imprints that we carry at a soul level from lifetime to lifetime.

According to various schools of Indian philosophy, every action, experience, or intent by a soul leaves a *samskara*, which is imprinted on the individual. These impressions are then activated through the individual's current life experience. In ancient Indian texts, the theory of *samskara* explains how and why we have past-life memories, and the effect that these memories have on our experience in this life, in both a positive and negative way.

YOUR SOUL GIFTS

On the next page you'll find a list of qualities or traits. Take a colored pen and circle the qualities or traits that best describe your *human self*. The part of you that consists of your body and your mind, your ancestral line, and your family of origin; it includes your inherited traits and you could say, your fated life, or the life you were born into.

Then, using a pen of a different color, circle the qualities that best describe your *soul self*, the part of you that's ancient. These are the qualities that you came in with – the traits that your soul has been working on for lifetimes. Your soul's gifts (things that come naturally to you, regardless of your upbringing) and you could say, your destiny life, or the seeds of destiny that were planted within you. The qualities and the life your soul is calling you to embody, follow, trust, and live.

Don't overthink it – trust the words to which you're silently drawn. Stay open to discovering hidden qualities of your soul and the difference between your human self and your soul self.

Courageous   Companion   Rooted
                                              Igniter
              Happy
Elder   Challenger
                                    Witch   Shy
      Joyful   Way shower
                              Visionary   Quiet

Unfathomable
   depths   Alchemist   Considered
                                  Calm
              Teacher

                    Midwife   Deep-Sea Diver
Abundant
         Healer   Energetic
              Excitable   Empathic
Powerful
                                  Lights up the room
                    Bright

    Cosmic
                          Questioning   Presence
              Beauty
    Activating   Generous
                 Catalyst
                                              Inspiring
Wise   Young
         Understanding
                          Adventurous   Blissful
         Ancient

                              Golden   Clear
Unrestrained   Wild   Elegant

Sage   Boundless   Sees the potential in
     Striking   everything

Embodied   Ready   Creative   Steady

     To the point   Sweet   Filled Up

                          Poetic
Effervescent   Compassionate

Luminance
Thoughtful
Weightless
Fiery
Generous
Wanderer
Funny
Helpful
Connected
Patient
Accepting
Fierce
Driven
Ambitious
Witty
Storyteller
Ready
Timeless
Mystic
Magical
Gentle
Love
Sacred
Here
Grounded
Dancer
Remembers
Effortless
Wizard
Fearless
Tenacious
Strong
Soft
Passionate
Traditional
Deep
Multidimensional
Spontaneous
Light
Balanced
Nurturer
Refreshing
Lover
Risk-taker
Devoted
Powerhouse
Curious
Divine Masculine
Playful
Fun
Divine Feminine
Enthusiast
Present
Grateful
Channel
Mother
Caring
Explorer
Father
Hearty
Nonlinear

△
YOU WERE NEVER
MEANT TO FIT IN

Don't waste this precious life trying to fit in. It'll never work and will be a waste of a life. Yours. Who you are is far more than you could even begin to fathom. You were never meant to fit in. Being you is the whole point.

Don't spend your days squeezing your uniqueness into a box-shaped world. Your soul needs room to breathe to be woven here. Let all of who you are spill over. Better than that – forget the box altogether. Who you are was never meant to be contained or restrained. You were never meant to fit in. Being you is the whole point.

Don't wish away your hours, weeks, months, and years dreaming of being someplace else. If you knew how many things needed to come together for you to be here right now, you'd dream of elsewhere no more. I know where you are can be challenging, and how painful it can be for your unique soul's arrival not to be celebrated and seen. You were never meant to fit in. Being you is the whole point.

Don't diminish your existence by desiring to be like someone else. Since the beginning of time, your soul and your body have been evolving into who you currently are. Ancient stars had to explode and gravity had to pull them to Earth, just so you can exist and breathe in this very moment.

You were never meant to fit in.
Being you is the whole point.

Child of the Earth and the Stars

Precious child of the Earth and the Stars.
Spirit Earthed in a rare moment in time.
Your soul went through a lot to be here.

Precious child of the Earth and the Stars
Nourished by your Mother, great birther of us all.
Protected by your Father, keeper of the stars.
Washed by your Grandmother, mover of the tides.
Warmed by your Grandfather, the one who lights up the sky.

Precious child of the Earth and the Stars
Cradled each day in the arms of your Mother.
Uplifted by the limitless vision of your Father.
Held in the nightly luminance of your Grandmother.

the unchanging
morn by rising
each of
your
Warmed _____ Grandfather

Wandering soul of many homes.

Forever dancing between forgetting and remembering.
Ever changing ever changing ever changing.

Seeded, planted here for but a breath in the
tapestry of what humanity calls time.

△
YOUR SOUL BIOGRAPHY

Inspired by the lectures of the Austrian philosopher Rudolph Steiner, Biography work is a discipline that develops self-knowledge by examining the great mystery of the human experience through the timeline of the years of our life. I've gotten so much from this powerful work, and in doing so I've extended it to the existence of the soul.

If the human life is a great mystery then the life of the soul is clearly even more mysterious, multifaceted, and deep. I call this work Soul Biography work, and over the years I've seen firsthand how remembering, uncovering, and claiming parts of who we are at a soul level can add to a fulfilling life, as it can help us connect to the part of us that never dies.

With Soul Biography work I intend to support you in connecting to the part of you that existed before you were born and will continue long after your last days, so that all parts of you can be fully grounded here. I believe that this inextinguishable part of you, of us, is connected to all of Life itself.

And that in connecting to this part of us we're also connecting to the Life force of all things. I believe that this part of us that's connected to all things is available to guide us each and every day. And the more we get to know this part of us and develop a relationship with it, the more in flow with the rest of Life we'll have the chance to be.

I must say now that from my perspective, the purpose of Soul Biography work is to call all parts of you here. It's not to spend your days longing to be someplace else; it's so that you can gather the confidence to claim your soul gifts and qualities in your current life. To truly be and do what you came here to be and do. I believe that any soul gifts, power, knowledge, or experiences are available to tap into right here and now, and that everything that your soul has experienced is available to you now. But, as always, it requires daily grounded action to embody and integrate.

The next few chapters will serve as a starting point for you to explore your own Soul Biography. If you're called to go deeper with your personal remembering, then trust that, and you may choose to find a skilled practitioner or teacher to support you in doing so. My online course Discover Your Cosmic Blueprint will also guide you through this process in more detail. You can find out more at www.rebeccacampbell.me/discoveryourcosmicblueprint. At the same time, if you're not genuinely called to go deep in remembering your soul history right now, trust that too. There's no greater authority than your own soul. Let that guide you above all else.

△
THE AKASHIC RECORDS

One way to access your Soul Biography, or begin to remember information about it, is through connecting to the Akashic Records. Early on in my career, I trained in working with the Akashic Records and through connecting to them, I supported my clients. I still use this connection in my own soul work, albeit in a less structured way.

The concept of the Akashic Records, also known as 'The Book of Life' or 'The Great Library,' describes a non-physical, multidimensional collection of every thought and piece of information that ever was, is, or will be. Many ancient traditions refer to the Akashic Records as a great temple or library in the sky, and within this great library we can find our personal soul book, which documents all of our past lives, current realities, and even future possibilities.

In his book *Edgar Cayce on the Akashic Records*, Kevin Todeschi writes that Cayce, a 20th-century American mystic, suggested that 'information about these Akashic Records – this Book of Life – can be found in folklore, in myth and throughout the Old and New Testaments. It's traceable at least as far back as the Semitic peoples and includes the Arabs, the Assyrians, the Phoenicians, the Babylonians, and the Hebrews. Among each of these peoples was the belief that there is in existence some kind of celestial tablets which contain the history of humankind as well as all manner of spiritual information.'[1]

The Akashic Records are referenced in both Western and Eastern mythology – the term Akashic comes from the Sanskrit word *Akasha*, which means 'boundless time and space.'

In working with the concept of the Akashic Records and our own personal soul book, we're able to access information relating to the history of our soul, our soul in this moment, and our soul in the future.

While many people in spiritual circles refer to the Akashic Records as existing in the fifth dimension, in Akasha, and say that it's through journeying to these different dimensions that we can access this information, I personally believe that once we've connected with the Akashic Records we can access them at any time, in a way that's similar to connecting with our intuition.

ACCESSING THE AKASHIC RECORDS

As with any soul work, I personally believe that it's very important to access the Akashic Records with deep discernment and energetic clarity. Always open sacred space before you access the Akashic Records and close the sacred space when you're finished, as it can become energetically draining to be connected to all of that information. Described below is how I open and close sacred soul space before and after doing energetic or devotional work.

OPENING AND CLOSING SACRED SOUL SPACE

To open sacred soul space, simply bring your hands into prayer position in front of your heart. Knowing that your palms are connected to your heart chakra, take a breath inward here and imagine your heart opening. I like to imagine a beautiful rose or flower opening in my heart space and opening more with every new breath. In the center of the rose or flower, imagine a light.

Inextinguishable. This is your soul, your ancient self – the part of you that's connected to the wisdom of the Life itself.

Next, allow your hands to travel upward in prayer above your head. Let them stretch out and travel around your body and then back to prayer. As you do, imagine that beautiful rose or flower opening all around you and the wise light of your soul growing bigger and bigger until it envelops all of you in a sphere.

To close sacred soul space when you're finished, simply do the same thing, but in reverse. Starting at your heart with your hands in prayer position, let them travel down to your root chakra and then gather the sacred soul cloak of light around your body, with your hands meeting in prayer just above your head. Next, let your hands drop down into prayer in front of your heart and have a moment of gratitude with your own soul.

Think of this process of opening and closing sacred soul space as opening a door when you arrive and then closing it once you're ready to leave. Tapping in and tapping out.

If you're accessing the Akashic Records yourself, I recommend connecting with and working with your Akashic Records Guide. You'll have an opportunity to connect with your personal Akashic Records Guide in the attunement I share on the next page. You can record yourself speaking the attunement out loud or visit www.letterstoastarseed.com to download the guided version of it.

AKASHIC RECORDS ATTUNEMENT

During this attunement and journey your body will remain safe, supported, and grounded as we invite your soul to journey to and from the Akashic Records.

Lying down or sitting upright with your spine straight, begin to get really comfortable. Gently close your eyes. Invite your body to enter a state of deep, deep healing and replenishment. Begin to feel the presence of a circle of light around your body, protecting it and inviting it to enter a state of deep healing during this journey.

As you bring your hands up and around and back to your heart, imagine that beautiful flower, and imagine that flower opening, petal by petal. In the middle of the flower is a light, representing your soul – your ancient self that's traveled from lifetime to lifetime and beyond. It is connected to all of Life. This part of you has wisdom beyond your years and knows exactly why you came here now.

As I count down from five to one, I invite you to begin traveling through the portal of your heart to your Inner Temple. Your Inner Temple is the access point to your inner guidance, through which we'll be traveling to the Akashic Records.

Five. Four. Three. Traveling through the portal of your heart to your Inner Temple.

Two. One. You now find yourself standing at the steps of your Inner Temple, looking up and being met by your Inner Temple Guide and Guardian. You walk up the steps and your Inner Temple Guide and Guardian opens the door and

*welcomes you to step inside. Crossing the threshold, you
see a golden cord anchored in the very center of your Inner
Temple, leading to a beautiful golden staircase on the other
side of the Inner Temple.*

*Your Inner Temple Guide and Guardian invites you to follow
this golden cord, this golden thread, toward the staircase,
and together you start to climb this staircase to the fifth
dimension, to Akasha, where the great hall of records
resides. Steadily you climb, up and up and up through all
of the dimensions, through time and space, to the fifth
dimension – to Akasha, the great library in the sky. The
infinite library of everything in the entire Universe, where all
information of the past, present, and future is available for
you to tap into; where Kairos time, timeless time, soul time,
wisdom time, reigns.*

*When you reach the top of the staircase, you and your Inner
Temple Guide and Guardian follow the golden cord to the
great library in the sky – the Akashic Records. You begin
walking up the steps of this great library, this great place of
records of all time and eternity, where you're met by your
very own Akashic Records Guide.*

*Your Akashic Records Guide welcomes you to the Akashic
Records and opens the door and leads you into the great
hall of records. As you begin to make your way down the
hall of records, you notice there are so many books. All
these books filled with information, documenting all the
things that have ever happened, are happening, or ever will
happen. These sacred, ancient books being updated every
single moment – ever changing as Life is being lived and
written and updated every moment of every day, as each*

individual soul weaves in and out of their lives and sings their unique song for another day.

Your Akashic Records Guide then leads you to a wing of the hall of records where your own soul book resides. You look around and see billions and billions and billions of books, each containing the unique records of each individual soul that ever was.

Your Akashic Records Guide then leads you to a section of the shelf and reaches out for a unique book, which you realize is your soul book. The book of your soul. The book that contains all the information of who you are as a soul. Your past, present, and future life experiences, and everything in between. This book contains all of the lifetimes you've ever lived. All of your soul gifts, all of your life lessons, your growth, your triumphs, your trainings – absolutely everything in the existence of you.

Your Akashic Records Guide now invites you to take a seat and to hold your soul book in your hands. Your Akashic Records Guide invites you to place your hands directly on top of the book and to breathe in the ancient nature of who you truly are. You take a moment to drink in your soul book. What do the pages feel like? You run your hands over the front cover of your soul book and notice the color, the texture, and the materials from which it's made. You notice any details. What's written on the spine? Is anything written on the front page? Is anything written on the cover? How thick is it?

Your Akashic Records Guide invites you to notice how old the book is, and with your hands and your palms being extensions of your heart you ask the book: 'What information do you have that is supportive for me right now and is in the highest good of all? What message do I most need to remember? How can I commit more to my current incarnation? What will help my soul to come all the way into my current life?'

Your Akashic Records Guide invites you to flick through the pages very briefly, to feel and notice the texture of the pages, to smell and to drink in with your senses even more of this book that documents who you are as a soul.

Knowing that you've connected with your soul book, and that you now know the way to it – through the great library and the great hall and to Akasha – your Akashic Records Guide takes the book and places it back on the shelf. Your Akashic Records Guide escorts you out of this section of the library and you retrace your steps, down the hall of records, past the billions and billions and billions of books. Feel how familiar this place feels. Your Akashic Records Guide reminds you that you now know how to journey here and tells you to return when you want to check in for guidance of the highest good of all.

Your Akashic Records Guide leads you out through the door of the great library of Akasha, down the steps where you're reunited with your own Inner Temple Guide and Guardian. You follow the golden thread with your Inner Temple Guide and Guardian back to the golden staircase. Down, down, down you climb, through time and space and different dimensions back to your body and through the portal of your heart. When you reach the bottom of the staircase, you find yourself back in your Inner Temple, following the golden thread that led you to Akasha, retracing your steps.

Now you know the way, you can return here whenever you like. Your Inner Temple Guide and Guardian leads you out of your Inner Temple, closing the door behind you. As I count down from five to one you'll find yourself traveling back to your body through the portal of your heart, back into the present moment and the room that you're in.

Five. Four. Three. Two. One. Very slowly, opening your eyes and coming back to the room, transitioning from Kairos time to Chronos time.

If you feel called, find a notebook and pen and write about anything you remember from your experience. This could include any visuals, feelings, whispers, information, or knowings. You may even like to draw any visions you received. Remember that everyone receives information differently, so trust your experience and stay open to receiving more as time goes on.

It's important for us to look at our past-life experiences with compassion, acknowledging that being on Earth can be extremely challenging because of the density of the energy and the polarity that exists.

If you're genuinely called to do soul work such as remembering past lives, it's important to take the soul work seriously by ensuring you're energetically safe and held by a skilled practitioner if you feel you need that holding.

△
PAST INCARNATIONS

The soul is the part of us that exists beyond this lifetime. It's our essence, our ancient self – the part of us that exists from one lifetime to the next. Each incarnation, and the experiences within it, craft who you are as a soul.

You're a multifaceted being, more unique than anyone could possibly fathom. The essence that breathes through you from one lifetime to the next is so precious and unlike anything else that's ever existed. Each of us is an ever-changing, impermanent expression of inextinguishable Life, constantly reinventing itself in an ever-unfolding expression.

Our past incarnations can include lifetimes spent on Earth as well as elsewhere. While the specifics may vary, most of the world's cultures and religions recognize the presence of the soul and many believe that the soul incarnates over and over again.

**Each life and experience adds to who you are
from a soul perspective. I believe that the
purpose of each incarnation is to truly incarnate.
To call the soul more and more fully in.**

As I shared in the chapter 'Meet Your Soul' on page 32, the soul carries karmic impressions, which are imprinted memories, gifts, vows, contracts, and experiences, and the Sanskrit word that forms the basis for this karmic theory is *samskara*. The *Monier-Williams Sanskrit-English Dictionary, 1899* defines *samskaras* as 'mental impressions or recollections; impression on the mind of acts done in a former state of existence.'

According to various schools of Indian philosophy, every action, experience, or intent by a soul leaves a *samskara*, which is imprinted on the individual. These psychological imprints or impressions are carried with us at a soul level from lifetime to lifetime, and they are then activated through an individual's current life experience. In ancient Indian texts, the theory of *samskara* explains how and why we have past-life memories, and the effects that these memories have on our experience in this life, both in a positive and a negative way.

It's easy in this current life and in this current world to see ourselves as good and bad. As one thing or the other. But if we can zoom out just a little we may get the smallest glimpse of the multifaceted note we play in this great orchestra of life. The cosmos is the organized Universe, and through the seeming chaos of this world, this life, and the polarity that comes with it, it's easy to lose sight of that.

It's easy to forget the incredible living, breathing miracle that you being here is, and how each and every moment, you're part of creation itself. That your authentic presence influences the outcome of Life itself. That what you do, what each of us does, has an impact, a ripple effect. That we're together creating the future from moment to moment to moment. That you being here matters – not because you're the center of the cosmos, but because you, like each and every being, are part of the very same cosmos. Cells within cells, worlds within worlds, universes within universes.

WORKING WITH YOUR SOUL'S PAST INCARNATIONS

Just as our current life experiences from day to day, month to month, year to year, influence who we are today and who we'll be tomorrow, our soul's incarnations and experiences shape who we are as a soul. And who we are as a soul influences who we are today.

Here are some of the reasons you may feel guided to embark on the soul work of remembering your soul's past incarnations:

1. To gain a deeper insight into who you are as a soul, so you can understand who you are today at a deeper level.

2. To call upon strengths, wisdom, or gifts, so you can gather up the confidence that may serve you with your soul's mission and journey in your life today.

3. To help you with your chosen life lessons or the challenges that you're currently facing.

4. To release energy from the past where you may be reliving a certain pattern or soul story that's stopping you from living in the moment today in this life.

5. To gain a deeper insight into a karmic relationship with a person, place, or system in order to face it and move through it so you can be more present in your life today.

It's believed that before incarnating, each soul carefully chooses the physical body, location, parents, and family that would best fit their karmic history, challenges, and soul missions (individual and collective). Here, we also choose our life lessons, which I'll speak about further in the chapter 'Life Lessons' on page 68.

I believe that we also make soul agreements with other souls to help us on our own personal and collective soul missions. I experienced this firsthand when I was regressed to the moment before my birth when I was receiving my own personal and collective soul missions (you can read more about this in the chapter 'Why Did You Choose to Come?' on page 99).

On the whole, it seems that most of us don't remember our past incarnations (from this world or beyond). However, there have been many documented cases of children who've remembered details from their prior incarnations and this information being proven to be true. Perhaps as babies and young children we do come in knowing, and this veil of remembrance stays open in some while gently fading in others.

Regardless, it's not uncommon for the awakening process to trigger an evocation of past-life memories. This has been my experience, particularly during the intense awakening period that I went through between 2011 and 2013.

While it's fascinating to discover this information about who you are as a soul and the unique journey your soul may have been on, it's also important not to identify with or get too lost in the 'story' of it; just as it's important not to get lost in the 'story' of our current life. For example, things like, 'I was a queen,' or 'I was burned at the stake,' or 'I was this famous person,' or 'I was an intergalactic High Priestess,' or 'this person betrayed me.' Past lives and in-between life experiences are in the past (they can also be in the future, but that's a topic for another book!)

If you're called to work with your past incarnations, there are many skilled practitioners who can support you in doing so; however, as with any kind of soul work, be discerning, and only ever do this work when genuinely led from within. There's a common misconception that soul work or light work is all warm and fluffy stuff. But in my experience, when it comes to proper soul work, this is in fact far from the truth.

In my opinion, it's impossible to be truly in the genuine light without continually facing our shadows. And the light is fierce, not just gentle and soft. The same goes for our current life. In my experience, those whose presence holds the most light have been courageous enough to dive into the depths of grief and the extremes that life brings. They're able to be compassionate because their hearts have been broken open. They've kept their hearts open through the greatest tragedies of their lives and as a result their hearts are open to experiencing the joys of life too. They are able to hold the poles of life all at once, never denying or bypassing the other.

Deep soul work often calls for us to keep our heart open as we swim through the shadows in order to reach the light. For this reason, it's crucial to do it in a space that's guided and held. And when doing so, ensure that we create a safe container – a held energetic space – something that's important in any kind of deep soul work.

If you feel called to remember any of your past incarnations or in-between life experiences, feel free to use the following activations:

REMEMBERING PAST LIFETIMES ON EARTH ACTIVATION

'I'm ready to remember any lifetimes I've had that are helpful for me to remember and are for the highest interest of all now.'

REMEMBERING LIFETIMES OTHER THAN ON EARTH ACTIVATION

'I'm ready to remember any lifetimes and experiences my soul has had in places other than Earth that are relevant and helpful to me today and are in the highest interest of all.'

REMEMBERING EXPERIENCES IN BETWEEN LIFETIMES ACTIVATION

'I'm ready to remember any experiences my soul has had in between my incarnations that are helpful and relevant to me today and are in the highest interest of all.'

If you feel called to explore your past lives through connecting with the Akashic Records, you might like to do the Past Life Soul Journey. Or if you'd like to take this work even deeper, the Discover Your Cosmic Blueprint online course is a great deep dive into all of these topics and includes resources on uncovering your past lives and who you are as a soul. You can find more information on both of these at www.letterstoastarseed.com.

SOUL INQUIRY

Do you have any memories of your past lives on Earth?

Do you have any memories of past incarnations in places other than Earth?

Do you have any memories of in-between life experiences?

△
SOUL MISSION

When I first trained in the intuitive mystic arts and began sharing my creations, it became very clear that one of my soul missions was to support souls that had come for a reason to remember why they had come, and to help them unlock the seeds of wisdom and remembering within them through my creations.

I started to see a pattern when it came to soul missions. I began to see that some souls had two missions – an individual soul mission and a collective soul mission. As I shared in the chapter 'What Is a Starseed?' I started to call this having a double mission. Perhaps you resonate with having a double mission too.

A soul mission is essentially a plan or a reason for being here. I believe that all souls incarnate have a personal mission. A personal mission relates to the individual's personal soul plan – this could be to learn and grow and experience themselves in a human body. As Earth is a planet of manifestation and creation, this is all part of the personal mission. Each soul comes in with their own unique personal mission and karma to play out. I believe that there's no one set path for each of us; rather, it's more like possible unfolding paths and these paths continue to unfold as we go through our life.

A collective soul mission involves many souls coming together for a common goal. This time in which we're living is one that's unlike any other, and I've come to believe that many of the souls who are alive right now have come here to influence the outcome of the future of planet Earth. For this reason, I believe that many souls incarnate right now have a double mission – a personal mission and a collective mission.

I believe that there are many specific soul missions within a collective mission and that we're led to work on these collective missions together. If you have a collective mission you're not working on it alone, for it's always a shared mission. This means that it's about finding your role or note to play, and playing it.

I find that this information is important for Starseeds to remember as many have a feeling that they need to 'save the world,' particularly early on in their journey of awakening. In my opinion, it's not the world that needs saving, it's humanity; we need to learn new ways to support each other, the Earth, and all her beings. Humanity starts with us. If we each play our part in our collective mission we're more likely to reach the outcome that we came here for.

We must stop trying to save other people and instead focus on returning to love, ourselves, the Earth, and each other.

As we really are living in a time between ages, there's much that's being dismantled. One of those things is moving from competition to collaboration; this is difficult for us to transition to because it's not what we're used to. If you're being called to collaborate, do your best to heal the part of you that feels as if you have to go at it alone; the part of you that feels like you're in competition. For this part of us is the part that keeps us separate and severed from one another. I know that it's hard to heal and transition from these old ways of being to the new ones. Many of these behaviors stem from childhood, so the more you focus on cherishing the child within, the more harmonious your relationships will likely be.

Through my work I've received visions of those with similar collective soul missions being carefully placed and planted in many different corners of the world. I've also met many old souls who yearned to be in closer proximity to those they consider their 'Soul Family,' with whom they share a collective mission. I talk about this concept in more depth in the chapter 'Soul Family.'

My own Soul Family is spread across four continents of the world – none of us even live in the same city. Sometimes this makes me sad because I long to be in closer physical proximity to them. However, I've seen that we each are holding a certain frequency in the part of the planet we've been born to or called to. Creating constellations, seeding, anchoring a particular quality in our own way.

You've been carefully planted in the soil of the corner of the planet where you are for a reason. I know at times it can feel like we're the only one in our family, in our community, in our city, but we're never, ever alone, especially in your experience of aloneness.

The world is waking up now and we must stay planted in the Earth. The more rooted we become the more grounded we feel. Now isn't the time to long for places other than here. Now is the time to seed what we came to seed. To remember that within the seed of your soul entire forests and rose gardens exist.

We all have a part to play in the Divine plan. It doesn't have to be on the world stage to be significant. One person's part is no worthier than another's. One person's part may be to mother their child and reparent themself in the process. Another's may be to gather women in circle each month, providing community and a safe space for others to connect and be. No path is better or worse, more important or less significant. We each have within us a seed that we incarnated to root and nurture and let grow.

STARSEED ACTIVATION

'I am ready to remember my personal
and collective soul mission.

I am ready to seed what I came here to share.

I am ready to surrender to my unfolding path.

I am ready to transition from competition to collaboration.

I am ready to fully plant myself here.'

△
COSMIC ORIGINS

I believe that ultimately, all souls come from Source and that who we are as a soul is influenced by all of our soul's experiences, with each experience creating an imprint on who we are from a soul perspective.

The more time a soul spends incarnating in a particular part of the Universe (for example, a planet, star system, or galaxy), the more they will be influenced by this place and these experiences. So, the more time a soul spends incarnating on Earth, say, the more at home on Earth they will likely feel; and the more time a soul spends incarnating in Andromeda, the more Andromedan traits they will likely have.

I know it's quite far out to be talking about different planets and star systems and so I want to ground it in a way that will make more sense, based on our experiences here on Earth. Think about someone who is well traveled. The more time they spend in a particular city or country, the more that place influences who they are as a soul. The nature, the weather, the culture, the people... all of these details influence who that person is today.

Take me, for instance: I was born in Sydney, Australia, and I've spent a lot of my adult life in the UK (living in London and Glastonbury). The more time I spend in the UK, the more the place influences who I am. My time in London has influenced me in ways that are different to my time in Glastonbury – the land, the culture, the people, the community, and so on. And the same goes for our experiences beyond this incarnation as souls – the more time we spend incarnating in places other than Earth the more these places imprint on us and influence us.

During my years spent doing soul readings I saw that most souls who have incarnated in places other than Earth have experienced more than one place. And the more time they spent in different places the more they resonated with the qualities of that place. For example, a soul that's experienced itself in Mintaka and the Pleiades will resonate with both places. The more time a soul spends in a place, the more their experiences in that place influence who they are, and the more they will resonate with that place as feeling like 'home,' even longing for it.

If you feel genuinely called to explore where your soul may have had experiences other than Earth, there are information sources out there on the traits that are associated with these different star systems, planets, and galaxies. You can also explore your own cosmic origins through your Soul Journey and Akashic Records work.

However, I want to reiterate the importance of not using this information to disassociate from your current incarnation here on Earth. As with past lives, remember that your cosmic origins may be varied, with each experience contributing to who you are as a soul now. Rather, use this information to claim even more of who you are from a soul perspective and to seed that here, now, in your current life today. We chose to be here on Earth now and so that's where our focus should be.

I believe we've barely begun to scratch the surface of our celestial ancestry and that there are countless more places that our souls journey to and incarnate in and on beyond Earth. Our planet and galaxy are just one of many, known and unknown. I believe that in my lifetime, and likely yours too, we'll make genuine connections with intelligent life and civilizations beyond what we currently know. I believe that we're planting seeds and creating pathways to be reunited with our Star Family members. And that we're living in the crucible of a whole new way of seeing ourselves, the world, the Universe, and our place in it.

The Starseeds know that they hold the entire Universe within them. And that the flower, plant, stone, and cell do too.

△
SOUL PATTERNS AND SHADOW WORK

Earth is a planet of polarity and while many of us are committed to our soul growth, most of us (myself most definitely included) have had lifetimes where we've gotten it 'right' and lifetimes where we may have gotten it 'wrong.' Just as in this life, we may have done things that we're ashamed of when we look back on them with the consciousness we have today. The human experience is about growth and we must remember our humanity when doing this work.

Proper soul work isn't all about love and light. On the contrary, it's deep work that often requires us to dive to the unfathomable depths in order to find the pearl. Just as we develop patterns through this lifetime, our soul does the same over its journey.

One of the most powerful things to work with in the Akashic Records is uncovering soul patterns and soul stories. These can be both positive and negative – light and shadow – just as in this human life. And just like most things on this planet. Night and day. Summer and winter.

In my experience, every person has had a variety of different incarnations, and while it's wonderful to explore our brightest 'greatest hits,' just as in this life, it's the shadow work that offers the biggest possibilities for transformation and reclamation, as it's these experiences that can keep us bound and repeating the same stories over and over again.

There's another reason why uncovering these soul stories can be helpful – in some cases, we may have chosen to incarnate at this time, in this body, and to a particular family, to break individual, ancestral, or collective patterns as well as our own soul stories. So, our chosen incarnation can be the perfect setup for us to face and shift a soul story.

Sometimes, we can also find ourselves reliving a particular soul story or pattern, even when our soul has learned the lesson. And through remembering or receiving information about the past life, it's possible to potentially free the energy and leave this soul pattern or story where it belongs, in the past.

Take a look at any patterns or stories in your current life that you think you're ready to release. Is there one that feels like it has an expiry date? Are you being called to unwind from it? When you name something, you claim it, and when you claim it you regain your power, which results in it no longer holding power over you.

When acknowledging old patterns, stories, or ways of being, it's also important to acknowledge how they've served you up until now. For example, a soul pattern or story of playing small, caused by a soul fear of being seen or sharing your voice, would have served you by keeping you safe.

Once you know this, you might also like to look at any changes you can make to reprogram this pattern or story from your life. Are there any repeating patterns in your life that you just can't seem to shake? If so, name them now, and if you're called, feel free to repeat one of the following activations.

SOUL PATTERN CLEARING (GENERAL)

'I release all old soul stories and patterns that are
no longer aligned with who I came here to be.
I carry the lessons, growth, and gifts, but
I no longer choose to live the same story.
May I be unbound, unbound, forever unbound.'

SOUL PATTERN CLEARING (SPECIFIC)

'I release this soul pattern and story now.
I carry the lessons, growth, and gifts,
but I no longer choose to live the same story.
May I be unbound, unbound, forever unbound.'

△
SOUL GIFTS AND
SOUL TRAINING

As the soul journeys on, it gathers with it soul experiences, and through our soul experiences come our soul gifts. Soul gifts are essentially skills or areas that our soul has devoted itself to working on. Just as in this life, the more we focus on developing a skill or working on a craft, the better we become at that skill or craft, and the easier we make it look. Indeed, those who appear to be an overnight success very rarely are, and the same is true from a soul-perspective.

Artists, poets, midwives, healers, space holders, mothers, leaders, activators, creators, decoders, warriors, dismantlers, growers.... What's needed at this time is for us to remember our soul gifts and training, to reclaim them, and to embrace them with grounded action. When we reclaim our soul gifts and honor our soul's training, we take our place in the tapestry of life. We reweave our way into the great orchestrated, cosmic dance of life.

Every soul has gifts – qualities that their presence offers the world. In my experience, we all come in with them and one of the greatest feelings is when we claim them and find our way home to sharing them in our own way with the world around us. This doesn't have to be in a way that's loud or big. I've seen many people stumble on their soul gifts and feel like they need to wait for permission and external validation to step into them. If you're wavering over something that deep down your soul knows, and which makes you come alive, trust the golden thread in the great tapestry that delivered you here now.

Once you discover your many soul gifts, it doesn't mean that you're a master and don't need to do the work. What it means is that your soul has devoted itself to this skill and so it may come naturally to you and feel familiar, and in giving yourself to these skills, time seems to stretch and your soul comes more fully in. Once you find your soul's path, devote your days in this life to remembering and working on the gifts and craft with devotion. I think it's important to say here that your soul is always calling you and so walking the way of the soul is not a one-time thing but an ever-evolving journey.

Let's say your soul has experience as an artist, with the gift of creativity. It doesn't mean that at the age of two you'll be another Monet, but it could mean that you find you're drawn to a particular style of art, that creating lights you up, that time seems to expand when you do it, and that working with your hands to create beauty and seeing what others don't, comes naturally to you.

When you find a soul gift that makes you come alive – that allows your soul to incarnate more fully – give yourself to this gift, to this craft. Show up with dedication and devotion. Cherish it like a precious jewel. Trust the Life force present there. You'll come more alive in doing it and as a result the world will come more alive too.

When I was a young girl, I was drawn to ancient mysticism and spirituality. I was reading books on death, dying, and the journey of the soul when I was fourteen. Nobody in my family was interested or even conscious of these topics and I had to look outside the life I was born into in order to follow this call. It took me many years to gain the confidence to trust this soul call, and a big part of surrendering to it happened when I realized that perhaps my soul had been training and working on this craft (the great mysteries, healing, creating, and writing) for lifetimes. Perhaps you have your own similar story?

HOW TO RECOGNIZE YOUR SOUL GIFTS

Often, our soul gifts whisper to us and reveal themselves in the following ways:

1. They're the things that come naturally to us.

2. They're the things that light us up and make us come more alive.

3. They're the things that make time seem to stand still and stretch. And we'd choose to do them even when no one else is looking, and regardless of whether or not we're rewarded for doing them.

4. Sometimes (but not always) they're the things that might be unexpected or require us to step outside the obvious path or plan.

The concept known as 'soul training' refers to the soul devoting itself to training in particular skills and also to the specific training that it undertakes between lifetimes. I've been shown places where my soul has gone in between incarnations to learn and receive training in particular areas. Perhaps you have too?

No one knows what your soul's gifts and soul training are better than you. Don't wait for permission – follow the invisible trail of what lights you up and makes you come more alive. The more alive you feel, and the more time seems to stand still, the more of an indication it is that your soul is present and here for this.

You came into this life with a clear soul plan and gifts that you've been crafting for lifetimes. This is the part of you that longs to be seen and is ready to emerge. If you ever feel unprepared or daunted by the path that's calling you, perhaps you've been training for this path, this moment, for lifetimes. You're so much more than the days that have breathed through you in this life. You're also all of the lifetimes and experiences that came before. All of these have shaped you – and continue to do so – and made you, you.

STARSEED ACTIVATION

'I call forth the soul gifts and soul training that I've received throughout all of my lifetimes. I'm ready to embody them all now, without hesitation and without fear.

I've been training for this for lifetimes.'

SOUL INQUIRY

What makes your soul come alive?

What makes time stand still for you?

What invites your soul to come all the way in?

If you were to guess your soul gifts, what would they be?

What is your soul calling you to step more into right now?

What is your soul calling you to give yourself more fully to?

△
LIFE LESSONS

If you look at life on Earth as being 'school for the soul,' then life lessons are the curriculum in which we enroll while we're here. Just as our journey through life isn't linear, life lessons aren't one-off classes but rather themes that we choose to circle, deepening our experience in them as we make our way around and around the spiral of life.

Planet Earth is a great initiation for the soul – it's an opportunity to experience who we are as a soul in a physical, separate body. It's also a planet of polarity. I see life lessons as the curriculum we enroll in, the themes we choose to experience in all of their polarity. For this reason, life lessons aren't only about getting it right or ticking a list once we 'learn the lesson' – they're also about experiencing them from all angles, in all of their polarity.

Each year the study deepens more and more. So, if one of your life lessons is clear communication, it won't just be about working on your ability to communicate clearly; instead, it'll likely involve both clear and unclear communication. For you to be on the giving and receiving end of all kinds of communication, and to truly live the theme of clear communication from all possible angles as you wind your way through the spiral of life.

For this reason it's so important for our peace of mind and well-being that we do our best not to look at difficult times or times of deep learning as 'getting it wrong,' as if we've somehow failed. From the perspective of the soul, no experience is ever lost or wasted if we instead see it as an opportunity for soul growth and a deepening of our own incarnation.

When you're having a hard time, or perhaps when a friend is going through one, it's comforting to see things from a soul perspective, as this reminds you or them that right now, your soul is most certainly growing and living. And that's a big reason we're here. If you're struggling, in pain, or frustrated, know that you're not alone in this. And perhaps growing (contracting and then expanding) is the whole point?

SOUL INQUIRY

Look back on your life and the different experiences you've gone through. What have been the greatest lessons in your life so far?

What have been the biggest themes of your life?

Is there a particular area of your life that you're finding challenging right now?

If you look at things from a soul perspective, what are you learning through this challenge?

SOUL AGREEMENTS AND THE CROSSING OF PATHS

Soul agreements are predetermined arrangements or contracts made between two souls to do something in a particular life – and sometimes they can carry over from lifetime to lifetime. Soul agreements generally occur between souls that have a karmic history with one another and have some kind of karmic match.

These agreements could be to support each other on personal soul missions, or on a shared collective soul mission, or as a way of working things out karmically between the two. Once the meeting happens, something is awoken in both parties. As with everything in this world, free will always reigns and so it does require that a conscious choice be made.

When we're arranging the details of our incarnation, it's common to make agreements with other souls we'll be incarnating with; these agreements are in a way contracts between two or more souls. A soul agreement could be based on a karmic connection that's resulted from prior incarnations; it could be one that's mutually beneficial – to help two souls in their life lessons or soul missions; or it could be based on the connection between the souls – for example, a member of your Soul Family who you choose to help on their soul mission by playing a role to support the destiny of their life.

Soul agreements are as diverse as life lessons. A soul agreement could be made between two souls, several souls, or even groups of souls like a large institution. An example of a soul agreement could be one between a teacher and a student, and within that relationship could be several soul agreements. The relationship could help the student to find their path, and accept their personal and collective soul mission, and it could also help them to grow through positive or difficult experiences.

Other soul agreements can exist between friends or family members, work colleagues, or even neighbors. For example, you may be born into a family that's been incapable of moving past a particular way of being, and you may have made a soul agreement with these family members to teach them how to do that. And through the challenge of doing so, you may be honing your own soul gift of doing just that – this crafting of your soul gift may be the initiation required for you to realize and step onto the path of your own soul's mission.

A soul agreement between a large group of people might consist of changing a system that requires many players to do so. The souls come together and play their part in this happening.

Relationships are one of the most incredible and complex parts of the human experience, and as a result they're the number one way we grow.

If you're living a life with an open heart, you can't bypass the highs and lows of relationships in this life. It's my belief that it's impossible to get through life without some kind of difficulty with relationships.

And because relationships are the number one way we grow, they're not meant to be all smooth sailing. Indeed, those who are closest to you, and potentially most connected to you from a soul perspective, could end up being the ones who hurt you the most. And it's the moments that crack us open the most that teach us the most.

△
SOUL FAMILY

Our Soul Family is made up of the souls that we incarnate with repeatedly with rhythm. Soul Family members are often here to help or support other members in fulfilling their soul missions (personal, collective, or both), by playing a particular role in their lives. The relationships with Soul Family members can be lifelong (for example, a mother, sibling, partner, or friend) or consist of just being in your life for a short period of time (a romantic relationship or a short-term friend).

The chance meeting with a member of your Soul Family could fundamentally change the trajectory of your life – it could hurtle you into deep growth or it could simply offer you some kind of support at a crucial time on your soul's path. Relationships with your Soul Family members are arranged prior to incarnating in this life.

You'll likely feel an instant sense of recognition when you encounter a member of your Soul Family. The feeling may stop you in your tracks as you try to place them; it could be a bit like déjà vu. Members of your Soul Family may feel deeply familiar to you and being with them may give you a sense of being 'home.' Or maybe they make you feel uncomfortable for no logical reason. It all depends on the unique soul history that you and the other soul share.

Meeting a Soul Family member usually supports your growth as a human being, and as a soul in some way, and helps you to 'check in' with where you're at on your soul's journey. I've had some amazing experiences of recognizing and being recognized by a Soul Family member.

The first time I met a member of my Soul Family was when I was a teenager. We both felt an indescribable and instant connection – even though this person was three times my age – and this meeting initiated my spiritual path and the work I do today. It was a challenging relationship to understand at the time, due to our age gap; however, looking back with the perspective of the timeline of my life I can see how this crossing of paths changed my life.

SOUL FAMILY ROLES

Some Soul Family members can be loving, supportive, and positive connections, while others can be more challenging – hurtling us into deep processes of healing and learning. And in many cases they can be both. Below are some of the many roles that members of our Soul Family can play in our lives. Of course, people can play more than one role at different points in time, but there's usually a role that stands out above the other secondary roles they may play.

The teacher

The teacher is a hugely important role in our lives, and there are many different ways that someone can act as a teacher for us. They might literally be someone who teaches, guides, or mentors us, or a keeper of a lineage that our soul or ancestry is connected to.

They might be a wise friend to whom we can always turn for advice or help with unraveling our challenges. They might be someone we learn from through the experiences we go through in our relationship with them – current or former romantic partners can often play this role in our lives, as romantic relationships often hold up a mirror to teach us about ourselves, our shadow sides, our woundings, and how we can grow.

The healer

Souls that act as healers for us often come into our lives when we've hit rock bottom or are at some kind of threshold. Their presence in our life helps us to stand at a threshold and walk through the gates of transformation in some way. Our experience of their energy can be activating or it can feel like steady, unconditional love. Connecting with them helps us to feel safe, protected, and cared for, no matter what we've been through. We may be going through a dark time and they may be our lighthouse – guiding us home to shore as we navigate the roughest of seas. The healer reminds us of our wholeness, potential, and strength.

The catalyst

The catalyst comes into your life to 'shake it up,' so they'll often appear (or reappear) when you're stuck in a bit of a rut, hungry for change, or ready for a new adventure. They also have a habit of appearing when we're perhaps going down a path that doesn't serve us, and need a wakeup call. They shine a light on a change that our soul is calling us to make. The catalyst doesn't tend to be a lifelong companion or friend; rather, they appear suddenly in your life, shake things up for a specific time period, and then become less prominent.

The catalyst helps us to see things in a new way by encouraging us to ask ourselves new questions. What do we really want? What are we really here for? What do we really think of the status quo? Their presence can feel fun, exciting, and exhilarating – and sometimes a bit frustrating and triggering, as they may not be the most dependable person! This type of relationship is often a soul agreement we make with a Soul Family member to help keep each other on course and continuing to grow. The relationship is not always easy but it does shake things up for the better.

The companion

The companion is a lifelong relationship, or at least a long-term one. When you meet someone who plays this role in your life, it's as if you see straight into each other's souls. This person makes you feel so deeply loved and appreciated, just for being who you are. There's a deep recognition between you, and just knowing that you have this person as a friend makes you feel more secure in the world – you'll likely both see each other as a 'rock.'

This is a very special connection with a member of your Soul Family, and when you find each other, you won't want to let go. So, no matter what stage of your life you're at when you meet this person, it's likely they'll become one of your best friends and sometimes even your partner.

The soul growth friend

The soul growth friend plays a slightly different role in our lives to the companion. These individuals are the friends we connect with on our soul's growth. They're like your 'spiritual partner in crime,' and they tend to be on a similar soul growth trajectory to your own. Sometimes you may find they're going through particular things at the same time as you, or you may find that one of you has already been through what the other is currently going through.

The soul growth friend is a support for your growth – the person you call when you're going through some sort of growth. They 'get' you more than anyone. They are always reminding you of who you are. Soul growth friends help us to stay connected to our path, our growth, and our reason for being here on Earth. They also make the journey less lonely and much more fun.

The challenger

While the catalyst may contribute to our growth by stirring things up and calling us on to a quest, the challenger is just that – someone who challenges us. Often the challenger will trigger us, and so if we pay attention to what's being triggered we have a huge opportunity for growth. Sometimes this takes the form of keeping us on our toes and encouraging us to up our game, but at other times this type of connection can feel very painful, as these are the people whose presence may cause us to doubt and question ourselves or feel unseen and misunderstood. However, again, there's often huge growth and learning to be had from these relationships, which can be agreements we made at a soul level before we arrived on Earth.

The way shower and map maker

The way shower and map maker is the leader who teaches you by example. They're your guide, and they pave the path for you. They may be someone in your life who takes the road less traveled, breaks the mold, or does things first, showing you what's possible. This is a hugely important role because they offer a map, a blueprint for you to say yes to the call of your soul.

You don't need to know someone personally for them to be a way shower for you – they could be a friend, a family member, or a colleague, or they might be someone in the public eye who you look up to and learn from. It's likely that someone who acts as a way shower for you is a member of your Star Family. It's also likely that, as someone who's committed to your soul's path, you're a way shower and map maker for others.

SOUL INQUIRY

Are there people in your life who you think could be part of your Soul Family?

What role have they played in your life and what role have you played in theirs?

How has the presence of these people in your life influenced your growth?

△
STAR FAMILY AND
SOUL CLUSTERS

I've been shown in my work that prior to existing as an individual soul, many and perhaps all souls have existed in what I call a soul cluster. At some stage, we each broke away to experience ourselves individually, and those who are part of your soul cluster are part of your Star Family. Perhaps, if we trace it back far enough, we were all part of the same star cluster, our souls originating from the same pulse of Life.

From a soul perspective, members of your Star Family are cut from the same cosmic cloth as you. Upon meeting them you'll likely feel a connection deep in the center of your very being. Time both passes quickly and stretches when you're with them. You feel more yourself with them than with anyone else.

You know that someone's part of your Star Family when you feel as if you're 'looking in the mirror,' because in a way you are. I'm not referring to any similarities in this life; what I'm referring to is a soul frequency or quality that can be felt when you look into their eyes and they feel instantly familiar and comfortable.

Meeting a Star Family member is activating; something is stirred within you that can't go back to sleep. Seeds of remembering are nourished by their presence and begin to grow and breathe through the protective shell.

Members of your Star Family will share a similar collective mission to your own. For example, to seed a particular frequency or quality on Earth. This doesn't mean that your role will be the same, although it could be similar; however, what's more likely is that your presence on Earth will work with theirs to weave a particular frequency here.

You'll work together even if this isn't a conscious thing. For this reason, they're absolutely not in competition with you. Any advances in growth by one Star Family member can be felt by all. If one is here to share their voice and gathers the courage to share their unique note, it can be felt in the soul of all Star Family members.

Some members of your Soul Family may also be from your Star Family. It's common for Star Family members to incarnate at similar times, to work with anchoring similar energies onto the planet.

Often, you'll go out of your way to help those in your Star Family, instinctively knowing it's part of your path.

I've been shown that on Earth, Star Family members incarnate in very specific places around the planet to form a sort of constellation of energy in order to seed what they came here to seed. It's not uncommon for Star Family members to long to be in closer physical proximity to each other; however, a cosmic web is being created through the physical weavings of where they're planted around the world.

Often this coincides with the Earth's crystalline grid, with each Star Family member seeding the particular codes into the Earth that they have been called to. Connecting with your Star Family members is possible energetically even if you've not met them. Or perhaps you're blessed to have already crossed paths with them and are connected with them through modern technology.

Being with your Star Family is deeply comforting and helps you to remember who you truly are. In my experience the best way to call in your Star Family members in particular is by embracing who you are at a soul level without waver and courageously letting the world see the real you. When you show the world who you are, your people, those who are cut from the same cosmic cloth as you, can feel it and see it and recognize you blazing from afar.

Spending time with your Star Family members feels like nectar. It feels like drinking in and being reminded of who you are. Members of your Star Family share a similar soul essence to you. Some Star Family members you'll meet physically and others you'll not; however, at some level you'll feel their presence and find a comfort in them being here. Sometimes you'll recognize members of your Star Family even though you've never met them – they could be famous actors, artists, or people in the public eye that you recognize and who hold a similar frequency to you.

When a Star Family member dies you'll likely feel it very deeply, regardless of how long you knew them, or whether you even knew them at all. A certain soul mourning or soul breaking occurs, allowing the qualities that they held on the planet to be received by those Star Family members who remain here.

I see this as a sort of passing on of the lineage; perhaps you've felt this when a member of your Star Family takes their last breath. I've experienced this with Star Family members who were part of my intimate life, a Star Family member with whom I was linked professionally, and a Star Family member who passed who I never met but whose work inspired me deeply.

HOW TO RECOGNIZE A
STAR FAMILY MEMBER

Here are some ways you can know someone is part of your Star Family:

- You share with that person a similar energetic quality.

- The person feels like 'home,' in a non-codependent way.

- You may share a similar joint mission.

- You feel as if you know and remember them from the moment you meet or encounter them.

- They feel instantly familiar, comfortable, and not in competition with you.

- Time both passes quickly and stretches when you're with them.

- They make you feel understood; it's as if they 'see' you.

- They're able to help you gain a broader perspective on your life.

- You feel more yourself with them than with anyone else.

- You both feel nourished by your connection in a way that you don't usually.

- It feels as though you're on the same team and as if life is weaving you together in some unknown way, even if you're not in close physical proximity.

- That person's growth can be felt by you and your growth can be felt by them.

From a very young age I knew that I was called to do the work I do now, but I spent a lot of my life in a spiritual closet and in hiding because of a deep fear of sharing my voice. It wasn't until I saw a photo of two Star Family members together (who I'd not yet met) that I knew it was time for me to finally actively answer the call of my soul. Their presence sparked a remembering in me that I could no longer ignore. I was connected to those two people when I signed my first book contract. Within months, several other Star Family members came in because I'd made myself visible and seen. It was a wonderful gift for gathering the courage to do something that had scared me so much.

Do you long to call in your Star Family and support team? People who get you at a soul level? People who are the same kind of weird as you? People who are your chosen family? Perhaps they're looking for you too.

STAR FAMILY ACTIVATION

'I call forth my Star Family.

Those who are here to seed the same frequency as my own.

I call forth my Star Family.

Those to whom I'm connected at the deepest level.

I call forth my Star Family.

Those who are from the same sacred places as me.

I call forth my Star Family.

Those who share my collective mission.

I call forth my Star Family.

Those who recognize me in an instant.

I call forth my Star Family.

Those who activate me just by their presence.

I call forth my Star Family.

Those who I activate with my presence.

I call forth my Star Family and seed even more of my own true nature right here and right now.

And so it is and so it is and so it is.'

△
SOUL LOSS

Through our traumas and difficult experiences we can encounter something known as soul loss. Soul loss occurs when a part of us finds it too painful to be here and fully present in our life and fragments from our experience. Soul loss is a way that the soul copes with traumatic experiences – it cuts off and disassociates from the current experience. It could happen through a variety of different experiences and is relative from person to person. Soul loss can happen during this current lifetime as well as during previous lifetimes our soul has experienced.

When an individual experiences soul loss it can feel as if not all of them is really here – that a part of them has checked out. It's possible to call this part of their soul to return through intention. Many shamans and medicine people work with soul loss and you can also call all parts of you back home. Now more than ever, we need to call all parts of us back home. To our bodies. To be present in our life. To incarnate all the way in. When we call parts of us back we reclaim who we are and embody our power. Our life begins to open up and we feel more like ourselves.

When we experience a cracking-open, a loss, a heartbreak, it breaks us open, creating space within our human self and our lives to be present with our soul. But sometimes we experience a loss so deep that it touches a karmic thread within the core of our soul. This is something I call karmic soul break (think heartbreak but for the soul). When this happens we experience a cracking-open, not just of our human self but also of our soul. When we experience karmic soul break, all rationality often goes out the window.

It's in this moment that we have an opportunity to heal something karmic, meaning some wound or memory that's been carried over from lifetimes by the soul. These are the hardest of lessons, the most excruciating, darkest nights of the soul. But if we stay with it, to find the courage to face the shadow of our Self and allow our inner winter to carry us through, we're able to heal something at the depths of our being. The part of our soul that was broken is now anointed with golden thread.

Begin calling home all parts of your soul by repeating the following invocation out loud three times. If you'd like to do this even more deeply, you can repeat this invocation every day for 108 days – light a candle and repeat the invocation as part of your daily practice for as long as feels right to you.

SOUL LOSS INVOCATION

'I call all parts of me back home.

I call all parts of me back home.

I call all parts of me back home.

Thank you thank you thank you.'

△
THE INTELLIGENCE OF THE UNIVERSE LIES WITHIN YOU

There's a mysterious force that governs all of life. An intelligence that tells flowers when to bloom and the tides and seasons when to come and go. That intelligence is seeded within you, too. It was there before you drew your first breath and it'll be there well beyond your last. It's the part of you that informed every cell what to do when you were in your mother's womb. And it's waiting to be activated within each and every cell now too.

It's harder to resist this intelligent force than it is to surrender to it. It's within every flower and every tree. It's what tells the rose to drop its petals and the passionflower to transform into fruit. In this day and age, we've forgotten that this intelligence exists within us. After burying the Goddess we went so far into the masculine, focusing on the glory of the logical mind over the magic of the mystery. If we're to transition through this old age and into the new, we must find our way back to the mystery that's seeded within it all.

We're separate in body but part of the same Earth. Earth is separate in planet but part of the same ever-expanding Universe. So often we become disconnected from remembering the mysterious intelligence, forgetting that the pulse of Life runs through each and every one of us, for we are Life incarnate for just a moment. We can feel isolated and as if we need to figure things out for ourselves – to rely on our individual strength. When we do this we cut ourselves off from Life itself. Things get out of harmony within us and around us.

You're being called to remember the intelligence that's within each and every one of your cells. To remember that you're a precious child of a loving, ever-changing Universe. That you have access to the intelligence – to all of the wisdom, the strength, the flow, and the qualities there ever were, are, or will be. And to remember that if flowers know exactly when and how to bloom, then you do too.

SOUL INQUIRY

How can you surrender more deeply to the intelligent flow of life?

What is ready to bloom within you?

△

EMBRACING YOUR HUMANNESS

No one is immune to life's pleasures and pains. Earth is a planet of polarity and sometimes being human is challenging.

The pleasures of this planet usher us into a state of pure bliss. The excruciating pains hurtle us into a state of separation and agony. And if we allow it, our heart is stretched and made stronger through both the pleasure and the pain. If we somehow allow our heart to stay open through the pain, our capacity to experience the pleasure will be even more increased. Yes, we're here to grow through both the pleasures and the pains. Nature shows us how not to discriminate between birth and death, summer and winter, spring and fall. All are necessary to what it means to be human.

Try as we will, we can't use spirituality or our intuition to avoid the pains of being human or to hold on to the pleasures forever. We came here for both. To experience both. The challenge is to do all we can to keep our heart open to both. This is what it means to truly live as a human.

SOUL INQUIRY

How do you resist your humanness?

Δ

The Codes of the Seeds

Seeds must be buried in the darkness
before they can bloom into the light.

Seeds can't even begin to bloom without
embracing the fertile void of the winter soil.

Seeds can't flower without first
outgrowing the constraints of the bud.

Seeds can't bear fruit without releasing their beauty to the Earth,
and letting go of the very thing about them that captivated others.

Seeds come in knowing exactly what to do, within them
they hold the potential of entire forests and rose gardens.

Seeds have within them an intelligent timing
that's connected with the intelligence of the entire cosmos.

We are all seeds.
Future forests and gardens waiting to be born.

Each of us holding the codes of a new humanity within us.
Change is our natural state.

△

THE SONG OF THE
ANCIENT SEEDS

The ancients knew much more about our connection with the stars than we do. Their pyramids, temples, and other places of worship, created in precise alignment with the stars, exist in all corners of the world. Trust what has been seeded within the ancient Earth. Hear the song of the ancestors past and future calling you to pave the way for a new humanity.

Step into your ancient knowingness. Be held by the rememberings of the Star Ancestors. Listen with your ancient heart and soul. Think with the part of you that remembers and knows. All ancient secrets are whispered forever in your ears. All mystic knowing blooms in your heart. All potent power pumps through your veins. The trees know, the rocks remember, the water holds, the soil has secrets to share. Earth is made of ancient stars and your body is made of them too.

This global situation we're in can feel hopeless and helpless. Wishful thinking isn't the answer. Love and light alone are not the answer. Love and light can't be seeded and embodied without first acknowledging what has been severed, what has been disconnected. Healing isn't possible without first acknowledging all of this. Total incarnation is not possible without this.

Now is the time for creative action. Instead of surrendering to the way things are, we must take guided, grounded action in order to bring about change. We must dig deep to find another way toward each other.

We're the dreamers we're wishing for, but dreaming alone won't work. We're the leaders we've longed for, but leading alone won't work. We need to remember the laws of the Earth, of the physical, by acting on the dreams in order to bring them into being. To reweave together the broken threads.

May you, may we all, trust the seeds of the dreams that have been planted within you.

May you, may we all, act on these seeds of dreams with grounded action.

May you, may we all, plant our dreams for a healed humanity.

May you, may we all, act on them each and every day.

Reach out to each other. Be practical. Be daring.

Be open to being rewoven.

△

You Arose

Veins like rivers
Breath like the wind
Blood like the tides
Tears like the ocean
Heart beating to the Mother's drum
Ancient exploding stars in every single cell

The flower knows
The stones do too
Won't you remember?
You were never perfect
You
never
fell

You *arose*

Heaven perfecting itself
Light seeded into matter
Always
only
ever
unfolding.

I REMEMBER

Why Did You Come Here?

△
THERE MUST BE
MORE THAN THIS

At some stage, Starseeds wake up to the realization that there must be more than this. Perhaps it's because they've woken up to the knowledge that they, we, hold the entire Universe inside of them. Perhaps it's a memory of an existence in which there was something more, something different, to the ways of now.

Perhaps this knowing was seeded deep within them and the remembering of that something is the exact reason they've come – to be part of the remembering, to be part of the conception of another way; building the bridge to another way of being. The Goddess knows that now more than ever we need another way.

Those who awaken abruptly may find themselves asking the question: 'What's the point?' Now, those who aren't questioning may take this as there being something wrong with the questioner, based on their inability to be quiet and just fit in and do as they're told. But perhaps there's nothing wrong with the questioner, and it's our society that needs the shifting?

As children we naturally wonder and question, but somewhere along the way we learn to settle for certainty. Many learn how to shut down their wondering, dreaming mind and cram it into a tiny box in order to fit into the world that already exists. In our attempt to control we stop living the question and instead live the answer that we know for sure. But living the question is the way to find your flow.

Living the question is the only way to stay true to your true nature, for nature is impermanent, forever changing, and we too are nature. To live the question is to follow the invisible trail that your soul leads you on. Perhaps questions were never meant to be answered in black-and-white ways; perhaps questions were meant to be lived into. Perhaps living the question isn't about finding a finite answer at all.

If you've woken up in the middle of your life, unable to keep walking the line, unable to live the same day over and over and over again, perhaps you're here to pave a new path. To find a new way. To build a new bridge, brick by brick, as you walk it. To question what's been left unquestioned in order to find our way back home to Earth, to our true nature, and to ourselves.

Perhaps the question is a door to a whole new way of living – to a whole new chapter on planet Earth. And through living into the question we pass through the threshold and find a way to create a whole new world. Birth isn't possible without death. Spring isn't possible without winter. And right now, we're in a global winter.

SOUL INQUIRY

What question are you living right now?

What is that question leading you to do today?

△
WHY DID YOU CHOOSE TO COME?

While I know that being a soul having a human experience can be difficult at times – living on a planet of great polarity and surrounded by so much devastation, as we are right now – I also believe that Life is a great adventure for the soul. That souls line up to incarnate into a physical body in order to experience themselves in the physical and truly incarnate here. That prior to incarnating, your soul had a dream and your life, this life, is a direct manifestation of that dream.

I personally believe that I came to Earth for both a personal and a collective soul mission (as I mentioned in the chapter 'Soul Mission' on page 54). Until I was able to find the words and concepts to wrap around that knowing, it always felt like there was something I was forgetting that I desperately needed to find. Part of my own path has been having glimpses of the journey of the soul, forever fascinated by what happens when we die.

In my first book I spoke about my first life-changing experiences, which happened during a past-life regression when I was in my early twenties. In the regression I was taken to the moment before my own birth, when my soul was deciding the details of my own incarnation.

I remember looking into a body of water-like substance before me, alongside beings that were there to support me in making a decision about where and when to incarnate, based on my soul's personal and collective mission. After making my selection I was taken to a massive, open, very bright space where many other souls were gathering too, in order to meet with a group of beings called the Council of Light.

While I couldn't see other 'people,' I could see and feel their energy, their souls as balls of buzzing, glowing light. It was hard to differentiate between the end of one soul and the beginning of another. It was like the best reunion you could possibly imagine. Some of these different souls' energies were familiar to me, as if I'd incarnated with them before.

As a group we were then given our brief for this lifetime on Earth by the Council of Light. We were informed that in this incarnation we'd be part of a mass waking-up in the Western world and a much-needed return to Goddess/Mother God consciousness and the rebalancing of the planet.

We were told that our missions would be deeply infused in us and that while walking our unique paths, we'd be sent people and situations that would wake us up from our slumber early in life. As one of us woke up and followed the call of their soul, it would spark a deep-seeded memory in another, regardless of how physically close we were to one another.

Once we were awake, it would change something in us. We were to follow what lit us up – and, in doing so, light up the world around us. One by one, as each person did this, it would cause a chain reaction of others doing the same and a potential mass-awakening. We all then received information on our choice of life and our own personal missions. I couldn't tell you if there were 100 or 100,000 souls there with me because, as I mentioned earlier, it was hard to differentiate one soul from another, as if we were connected in our collective mission at this time. I saw how many of the souls were grouped together in waves, incarnating in unison over different periods of time.

Since writing about this soul experience and memory I've received hundreds and hundreds of letters and emails from people saying that they were there too. Some remembered this experience through reading my recollection, while others had already remembered it through their own exploration. Maybe you were there too? Or perhaps you're here with a different collective mission. Regardless, I do believe that there's a reason you chose to come, to be here now.

SOUL INQUIRY

Why did your soul choose to come at this time?

△

WE ALL HAVE A ROLE TO PLAY, BUT ONLY WE KNOW WHAT OUR ROLE IS

We all have a role to play, but only we know what our role is. Paths unfold only when we walk them. Don't let someone who is not you tell you what you should do. They're not you and you're not them. They don't know and will never know what's for you, just as you don't know and will never know what's for them. If they're spending their precious moments on Earth worrying about what you should be doing with yours, they're wasting theirs. Don't let them waste yours.

Your life and your time are precious jewels. If someone thinks that it's their job to point out the way your path should be spiraling, they're likely ignoring the jewels of their own life. Don't let their distractedness distract you from yours. Keep your gaze set. Politely invite them to do the same.

As you walk your spiral you'll find yourself turning toward others and others turning toward you. What a wonderful thing, to share your journey. And while your path may naturally influence another's, keep walking your way when the inevitable call to turn comes. And it always comes. Endings are necessary for beginnings to happen.

As you walk your spiral you'll find that others' spirals may overlap and activate you along your way. Let them. But don't let seeing someone else's potential unfolding convince you to boycott your own. This won't help you or them. Keep walking on.

Don't let someone who is walking a different path to your own tell you how to walk yours.

Nobody but you can or will ever know what it takes, has taken, and will take to walk your way. Wave them on, and without waver, keep trusting the seeds that have always been planted deep within.

SOUL INQUIRY

What are you being called to turn toward?

What are you being called to turn away from?

△

THERE YOU ARE

The greatest gift you can give another is to truly see who is there, behind their eyes. To see the great journey their soul went through to be here, Earth-side. To see the precious seeds planted deep within. For many, this is the original wound – to be unwitnessed upon arrival. Whisked away and placed on the conveyor belt of the life they have been born into. The soul squeezed into boxes. Into angular shapes.

Give the people in your life the greatest gift of all. See the ancient seed that blazes behind their eyes. The presence that existed before their body did. Witness the courageous quest of the presence that will journey on and on.

And even better than that, do what you can to show this part of you to the world. To let this part of you, the eternal part of you, be seen from afar. Don't hide it away. Don't wait for those who have eyes to see it to come looking for it. Show it to the world now. Don't squeeze it into boxes and shapes that could never hold the song that you came here to sing.

Don't contain it. Express it. And share it now. If you do, your people will hear you a mile off, and begin to sing along. Your soul is a beacon. It's your homing device. Let yourself be seen and call your people home to you.

SOUL INQUIRY

How can you let more people see the real you?

△

I Have Music in My Heart

I have music in my heart.
Ancient mantras echoing in all four chambers.
I have music in my heart.
Harmonics reverberate from bone to bone.
I have music in my heart.
Melodies that whisper from just behind the veil.
I have music in my heart.
An inner rhythm pulsing through my veins.
I have music in my heart.
Choirs of angels so grateful to be here.
I have music in my heart.
Monks, siddhas, and shamans clapping through the ages.
I have music in my heart.
A unique note that I came here to sing.

△

FINDING OUR GROUND

Many of the souls incarnate on Earth right now have been incarnating on Earth for some time, returning over and over again in an attempt to influence this very time we've woken up to. Some have been awakening from their slumber earlier than others, in preparation. Others have been abruptly ripped from their sleep.

This time that was long ago predicted is actually here. Today, tomorrow, the day after. These are those days. And we're waking up more and more with each coming one.

When you wake up it can feel disorientating, and difficult to find your ground. Yet the more grounded you remain during these changing times, the more helpful you'll be. Be dedicated to finding your ground – to calling all parts of you fully here.

The calmer you feel, the calmer others will feel around you. The steadier you feel, the steadier others will feel around you. The safer you feel, the safer others will feel around you. At this time of great change, we must work harder than ever to find our ground.

STARSEED ACTIVATION

'I fully commit to being here.

I call all parts of my mind, my body,
and my soul to this moment.

I show up each and every day to what grounds and calms me.'

△

STARSEED ROLES

I believe that in naming and claiming our soul gifts, discovering the role/s we came here to play, and understanding who we are from a soul perspective, we can feel a deeper sense of relief and purpose in the world. Thus, our quality of life and joy is increased.

We are multifaceted beings who have been crafting our soul gifts and who we are for lifetimes. Each of us has a completely unique array of gifts, a diverse soul history, and our very own individual path. If we were able to see these qualities from that perspective, we'd never feel as if we're here to compete with those who walk alongside us.

From the thousands of souls I've worked with over the years who resonate with having an individual and collective soul mission, I've come to see there are common roles into which Starseeds fit, and skills they have when it comes to their collective mission. Discovering our role and our soul gifts is so liberating. In my experience there's nothing more frustrating than feeling called to serve but not being sure how best to do it.

We can have many different skills, but we're not here to do it all. We're each completely unique and the best way to fulfill our purpose in the world is to express that in our lives. This doesn't necessarily mean we need to express our roles or gifts in the traditional sense, as a career – we can express them in non-traditional ways too.

Because this is a world of polarity (and it's through the extremes that we grow the most) each Starseed role has both a positive and a negative – the positive being the gift and the negative being a potential challenge. It's also important to acknowledge that we live in a world of free will and thus have a choice to use our gifts for the highest intention for all, and the planet, or for our personal gain alone.

Below is a list of the roles that I've found many Starseeds have. I share these not to limit your treasure trove of gifts, but as a process to help you claim them and find clarity and focus in your life. You'll find information about the soul gift and potential challenges that some Starseeds may experience. Because we are multifaceted beings with many gifts to share, we may find we're called to express ourselves in more than one way at different times.

ACTIVATOR

The gift: The activator ignites change in the world. They spark shifts in their relationships, community, and the world. The activator can help others be inspired to take grounded action. Their presence shifts things.

The challenge: Activators are very powerful – so powerful that sometimes their approach is a little harsh for those who are more sensitive or slower to see the big picture. Activators are great at getting the energy for something going, but they may need support in carrying things out.

ALCHEMIST

The gift: The alchemist turns all that's stuck, stagnant, and heavy into gold. They're not afraid to go to the depths. They're here to create huge shifts in the world and their presence alone can do this. They're the deep-sea divers of the world, devoting their lives to polishing the crystal and finding the pearl in the darkness.

The alchemist can work through alchemizing their own sufferings into gold; they can then also go on to guide others to do the same through their work and whatever skill they choose to devote their life to. Because they've gone to the depths, walked through the fire, and returned to tell the story, they have a capacity to hold people in deep compassion and guide them to do the same.

The challenge: Not everyone wants to look into the shadows, and as a result the alchemist's presence and gift may scare others. They may need to remember to ease others into the unfathomable depths and to know that not everyone is willing to do the work that they know they can support them in. Because the alchemist must first journey to the depths and walk through the fire, they'll likely go through a very difficult period in their life in order to do that. This is like a death and a rebirth in order to return with the gold of their gift.

ARTIST

The gift: The artist dreams a new world into being through their creations and the sharing of their unique vision. Their tools may differ – from writing to painting, from gardening to cooking, and from decorating to singing – but the artist brings harmony to the world by bringing things together to create beauty and inspiring others to feel and think differently.

The challenge: The artist's challenge is to trust in their gift so they can realize it. Gathering the confidence needed to focus on their craft is difficult for some artists, especially if the expression of their gift isn't traditional. The artist must focus on their craft in order to master it, and the creative process is often a solo gig, so they can be lonely while thriving in their creative caves. For this reason, developing a community of others who can support them along their journey, as well as midwives to help support their work in the world, can be important.

BIRTHER

The gift: The birther is here to usher in new worlds and ways of doing things. Birthers shift things through channeling new creations, information, systems, or other things that will influence the way the world works.

The challenge: The challenge for birthers is that often what they're here to birth is so huge, it can be overwhelming. They need to learn to call in support and then *allow* themselves to be supported in order to birth the new into the world, and also birth a new world. Birth requires labor and contraction as well as expansion, and so remembering this can help when going through times of contraction.

CHALLENGER

The gift: The challenger sees things differently. They're here to dismantle systems and open people's minds – to ignite and shift things. They may find that they fight for the underdog or a cause that's been overlooked and underserved. Challengers are here to inspire action and lasting change. They hold the vision for a new world.

The challenge: Challengers may find it frustrating when the rest of the world can't see what they see; and worse, that they *do* see it but aren't willing to do what it takes to bring about change. They may find it difficult to remain open-minded or patient around those who are closed-minded and unconscious. When their cause is so urgent, it can be difficult for the challenger to remember that everyone has their own unique role to play.

GRID WORKER

The gift: The grid worker is called to particular parts of the planet to be a guardian for the crystalline grid of the Earth. They act as energy workers for the planet and sometimes are conduits for galactic activity too, working with the crystalline grid of the Earth and sending information back and forth like a transmitter. Grid workers can be born in a particular town or city, or they can be called there to hold a particular frequency on the planet. I've met grid workers who were taxi drivers and had never left their particular town. I've met others who are very consciously called and actively do energetic work with the crystalline grid and power points around the world.

The challenge: The grid worker works energetically and so when the energies are more intense they may find that they become energetically influenced. Particular places on Earth can be energetically active and therefore grid workers need a way of letting the energy move through them, and take time to clear themselves, so they're not mistakenly carrying anything that isn't theirs.

HEALER

The gift: Healers see the wholeness in people, things, and situations. It's through holding the vision of wholeness that the other is able to see that too. People enjoy being around balanced healers because they generally feel seen and heard by them. Truly witnessed. Healers have huge hearts and a great capacity for compassion and understanding. They often find that people feel safe around them and may find that they share their secrets and truth with them more than with others.

The challenge: Because healers see the wholeness in all things they may find that they fall in love with potential rather than reality. This can express itself in relationships, where they fall in love with the potential of a person or a situation rather than the fulfilled reality. Healers often need to work on boundaries – to be clear on whom and how to devote their time and to recognize that healing cannot happen without the other person: That is to say, it's not them doing the healing, but rather it's holding the other in wholeness and then the other choosing to step into that.

MIDWIFE

The gift: Midwives are the support team – they're there to help birthers, artists, challengers, alchemists, visionaries, and activators to create lasting change in the world. Their constant support, holding, and grounded action make it possible for new worlds to be dreamed into being and lasting change to happen. They're all about grounded action and energetic support, even though they may not realize this is what they're doing. Midwives are much more comfortable in the support role than leading the way.

The challenge: Because midwives are supporters it's important that they don't lose themselves or their sense of self by over-serving. In order to create lasting change, and be able to do this work in a sustainable way, midwives need to find a way to replenish their own well.

SPACE HOLDER

The gift: The space holder is here to be a holding force in the world. Their presence alone changes things energetically. They're the ones whose presence encourages and supports others as they find their way through difficult times. The space holder tends to come into people's lives when they need it most, to process and step into the next stage of their soul mission.

The challenge: Space holders may find it hard to describe what they do, as a lot of their work is done without their realizing it. It's also important that space holders receive support, as well as giving it to others. Staying in touch with their body and their feelings is something that's important for space holders, in order to ensure they're not continuing to carry things in their body energetically.

VISIONARY

The gift: These are big picture thinkers – visionaries who can see patterns and the shifts needed to usher in a new world. Visionaries are the ones who are here to dream a new world into being. They'll see the way things could be, and can sometimes feel as if they were born before their time, because in a way they're here to create the future through their clear vision. They show people what's possible.

The challenge: Because of their ability to see things before they exist, it can be challenging for visionaries to trust their visions, as by their very nature they won't always be welcomed by the masses. This requires faith, so having people who support and encourage their visions is necessary. Visionaries see things clearly and to them it can be frustrating when others cannot.

SOUL INQUIRY

Which of the above do you resonate with the most?

△
BEING A CLEAR VESSEL
IN TIMES OF CHANGE

No one can get a clearer reading on who you are and what you're going through than you. This is why we're called to dig deep in times of change. It's more crucial than ever to stay grounded and be surrounded by people who champion your own inner knowing, your own inner wisdom, and your soul's ability to journey through this. And to venture into the underworld knowing you'll return changed yet even more yourself.

When we're going through initiatory times it can trigger us to feel helpless and alone. Those around us (especially those who love us the most) will always have an opinion, and while it may come from a loving and genuine place, it'll ultimately be colored by that person's own experiences, opinions, emotional reactions, and motives, as it'll either be coming from their ego or their own inner channel.

While it can feel helpful when we're desperate to be told what to do, being plugged into other people's channels often leads to frustration and confusion. It can take us off path, only delaying what we've tried to bypass or avoid facing. It can also make us feel even more alone as we separate ourselves from our true path of the road less traveled.

In times of change, and any time really, it's important to be plugged into your own inner channel above all else. Where possible, be clear on the guidance that you're open to receiving. Be discerning about the opinions you seek. Decide who will be on your advisory committee. Be clear on the support you'll need. Let them know what would be helpful and what would be confusing and harmful. And remember, ultimately, there will be no better knowing than the inner knowing you'll come to once you've gathered your information. Always, always, tend to your own inner channel.

SOUL INQUIRY

What are you avoiding facing right now?
What do you wish wasn't true?

△

THE VEIL HAS BEEN LIFTED

This era is one of uncovering mistruths so we can remember universal truths. It's one of realigning to nature to ensure this planet will be a place that souls can return to for times to come. Everything is in a state of recall and realignment. Anything that isn't in harmony with nature itself won't survive. Anything that's attempting to manipulate or divide and conquer won't survive.

We must align ourselves with nature and our lives with our own true nature. We must align our bodies with the rhythm of Earth and thus the Universe.

We must align our outer lives
with the inner guidance of our soul.
To surrender to the never-ending
beating of the great cosmos itself.

This goes for society and the world at large, as well as in our own lives. Some of us who are on Earth right now are here to lift the veil between the seen and unseen worlds once more. We're here to shine a light and thus cast a shadow on things that are inauthentic or unaligned with the survival and well-being of planet Earth. To stand for and protect those who don't have a voice, and to look deeper and question everything that previous generations did not.

We can no longer tolerate things that aren't congruent. We're here to bring society and humanity back into harmony with the planet and the cycles of Life at large. If we tolerate things in our life that aren't aligned, we add to the misalignment of the planet and ultimately separate ourselves from the Earth and the force of Life.

You're being called to trust yourself, to trust what hasn't felt right, to trust your body, and to trust your senses. That's really what it means to be sensitive – to have our senses clearly speak to us. It starts with a whisper, then an uncomfortable feeling, then a raised voice, and then a shout. By the time it turns to a shout the body lets you know. What have your senses been trying to let you know? What has your body been trying to let you know? Pay attention to your senses because they don't lie.

If we all did this, the planet wouldn't be in the state that it is. But we can start now. We can show up each day and listen. Every time we do that it makes a difference. Trust your senses. Your sensitivity is sacred; it's how Life and the soul communicate. You're not a victim of it – it's a strength that's waiting to be owned.

SOUL INQUIRY

What have your senses been trying to let you know?

What has your body been trying to tell you?

What isn't congruent in your life right now?

What action are you being called to take?

△

On Questioning Everything

The biggest challenges are designed at first to
separate you   from your faith.
Let them.
Don't judge yourself when you question it all.
When you doubt your beliefs, your devotion,
your God/dess, your entire existence.

It is in these times that we're meant to question everything.
It doesn't matter how long you stay away.
How much you ignore your faith.
How tightly you close your heart.
How long you dwell in your

s   e   p   a   r   a   t   e   n   e   s   s.

Each challenge is an opportunity to deepen.
But first we might retract.

the surface before diving once more to the depths.
to
up
Come

Eventually you will return to the pearls.
Waiting for you even deeper than before.

△
WEIGHT OF THE WORLD

You are not personally responsible for the way the world is. You don't need to personally carry what you didn't create, even if you're here to change it. Especially if you're here to change it. And we're *all* here to change it.

If we're to truly do the necessary work of change in these times we must prioritize our well-being. Put your body first so that you can do this work for a lifetime, not a season. If you're looking for permission to put yourself first, let this be it. You're no good to anyone if you're running on empty and in a state of overwhelm and inaction.

In these changing times, it's hard not to feel overwhelmed by the state of the planet, or by the unending list of systems and ways of being and tragedies to mend and fix. However, you can't take on the planet's problems from a place of energetic depletion day after day after day and expect your human body to be okay. Rest is necessary and looking after yourself is important.

Planet Earth has its seasons and your body is the Earth. You must honor the seasons of your body if you're to stay on the path year after year after year. It's not possible to be in full bloom all year round. Give in to your inner winter so that new seeds can come in. Let those seeds bud and bloom, blossom and fruit. Allow other voices to carry while you recover and rest. For they too will need to surrender to their own winter when the buds within you are once more ready to emerge and then bear fruit.

Only you know what you need and only you are in a place to give it to yourself. This isn't to say you should switch off from the world's problems and become unconscious; rather, it's a call to establish clear boundaries so you're not constantly taken out energetically. The planet needs you healthy – physically, emotionally, mentally, energetically, and spiritually. We all came to ride the waves of Earth's great oceans. Trust the one that you came in on.

SOUL INQUIRY

What are you carrying that isn't even yours?

What does your body need on a daily or weekly basis in order to thrive?

△
A TIME OF GREAT
CHANGE AND UPHEAVAL

This period in which we're living is a time of change, transition, and healing – both on an individual and a planetary level. The planet's changing at a cellular level and so are we. This lifetime is the result of many. This is the time we've been incarnating for. This is why we returned.

Mystics, wise ones, healers, witches, artists, change makers, drummers, singers, music makers, dancers, weavers, and visionaries of times past. Here to remember. As we each uncover this remembering we add our piece to the collective puzzle. Our step in the dance of Life.

As part of the transition team from one age to the next, you're at the forefront of this planetary transformation. To *transform* means to change form; the Earth herself has been changing in form, and we, in bodies, part of the Earth itself, are changing in form with Her. We've forgotten that law of nature, that ever-changing natural state.

This change isn't only happening externally – we're all changing at a cellular level too. This can be painful, but what makes it even more painful is resisting it. Attempting to swim against the tide. And the tides are changing each and every day. The Great Mother and the Grandmothers are busy weaving the threads of your life when you surrender to Her flow. Her cycles. Her inhales and exhales.

If you allow yourself the time and space to give yourself the nourishment and space that you so crave, watch as time expands.

We're changing our relationship with time and being right now. Don't you feel it?

Earth is slower than many souls are used to, and She's calling us to return to Her cyclic sync. We have to go back to go forward.

You're not here to save anyone but yourself; no one else is here to save anyone but themselves. We must become responsible for our own actions – in the past, present, and future. As each of us transitions from one age to the next – as we dance with the patriarchal shadows and shake off those ways of being that once served us – we set ourselves free. We unbind ourselves from the cage of the past and we realize that we each truly do have the key.

As you're alive on the planet right now you're on the frontline of a group of souls who have the potential to bring about a planetary shift of the ages. This shift, this rebirth, isn't a given, but it's a possibility. There's no question that these times, these changing times, require great courage. Have faith and find strength in knowing that you're not doing this work alone. You're called to be a midwife for a metamorphosing humankind. No one is exempt.

I know this work isn't easy. That's why not everyone is willing to do it with their eyes, mind, and heart open. As you dance through your own times of healing, know that it's not being done in isolation. Your personal work does affect the collective, just as the collective influences you personally. No cell or organ in the body works in isolation. Every person who frees themselves frees humanity a little more. Every person who heals themselves heals their ancestral lines a little more. New seeds of freedom are planted, and those seeds, with the right nourishment, have the potential to create a whole new humanity. Please may it be so.

△

IT'S TIME FOR THE SONG TO BE SUNG

The world is far older than our documented history suggested. The mystery far more unfathomable. The dust of the ages far more deep than is documented. The wisdom waiting to be found. As souls, many of us have experienced ancient eras on this planet that were much more advanced than ours today. We've witnessed the rising and falling of ancient civilizations and lands lost to the winds of time. As we begin to recall these times, the rememberings, wisdom, and gifts can come flooding back. The Great Mother knows we need them now more than ever in order to avoid repeating past mistakes.

At this stage in Earth's timeline, we need the wisdom of the ancients in order to survive as a species. At this stage in Earth's timeline we need to birth a new humanity in order to survive as a species. You're being called to connect with the lost wisdom of your ancient soul and your ancient ancestry. To reach all the way back to the Original Mother. To dig deep and bring forth the seeds planted within you. To remember what has been imprinted so we can collectively find a way. To scatter those seeds and tend to the garden of your ancestral line all the way back and all the way forward.

If you feel unprepared, perhaps this is the exact reason you came. Perhaps your soul has wisdom beyond what your lifespan can imagine. Perhaps you've been preparing for this time; perhaps we all have. The curtains are drawn, the show has begun, the orchestra is playing. It's time for the song to be sung.

STARSEED ACTIVATION

'I unlock any forgotten wisdom and
soul gifts from lifetimes past.

I reach back to the Original Mother and call upon
the strength and support of my ancestors.

I trust and tend to the seeds planted within me.

I let the ancient Grandmothers of the Earth –
past, present, and future – sing through me.'

△
YOUR LIFE IS A CANVAS

In many ways our overly capitalistic society has led us to believe that we must consume, not create. We've forgotten that we're all artists and that this life, our life, is the canvas upon which we create. We've been taught that creativity is something that exists only within some people – a rare gift, a certain specialness. But creativity isn't limited to some of us, it's within each and every one of us, and that means it's within you too. Creativity and intuition come from the same place, and that place is where the soul resides.

Earth is a planet of manifestation, a place where we came to create. What kind of world do you want to create for those who will come after you? What are you being called to create with this Earth? It's never too late to start, and no experience is required. All you need is an open heart and mind and consistent daily action.

The reason why people don't trust their creativity is twofold. Firstly, many experienced a shutting-down of their natural creativity at some stage during their childhood. A mean or thoughtless comment from a teacher, parent, sibling, or peer created a severing from one of the most natural things in the world – our ability to create.

Secondly, many of us spend too much time thinking and not enough time taking grounded action. In the years I spent working as a creative and creative director and then in my workshops, I saw it over and over again – people who were overwhelmed by too many ideas and worried that if they didn't have the right idea or feeling they had to wait to see the step-by-step detailed plan.

There are books and songs, inventions and innovations, sculptures and world-changing ideas that are waiting to be ushered onto this planet. Solutions to problems that we don't have time to wait to fix. As creatives we must stay in the wonder and the trust. Live in the adventure and the uncertainty. Dive into the flow of life and trust that the next step will be revealed at just the right time.

If you have an idea or a creation that's beckoning to be born into this world, be sure to properly seed it into the Earth with grounded daily action. Keep showing up to your creations and your craft each and every day. If you do that, what you're being called to create will take root, bud, bloom, and fruit. And if you allow yourself to rest, come winter, your creations will be born again each and every spring. Trust that you'll be led, and eventually you really will trust that you'll be led.

SOUL INQUIRY

What are you being called to create?

△
CREATING IN TIMES
OF CHANGE

I know that in these times of great change it can feel especially scary to create. With the need for and sometimes the impossibility of nuance. To put yourself out there with the risk of being shut down or getting it wrong. To share your truth and then moments later wake up a little bit more and realize that the pendulum of consciousness, both within and around you, has swung some more. To use the privilege of your voice and let yourself be sung, not knowing how you'll be received. To run the almost certain risk of, at some stage, being misunderstood or getting it wrong.

When the artist creates they put into matter what is felt in the hearts of many. When the artist creates, it helps others to make sense of the ever-changing world.

As a creative, it's normal to look back on your past creations and want to change them, perfect them, even destroy them; to make them, like you, a never-ending work in progress. But that's not the role of the artist, of the creative, of the poet, of the writer, of the mystic, of the healer, of the weaver. We didn't come here to find out the answer and then create that. We came here to live it, to feel our way through it, to dance it, and to sing it, to write it out. Together we may just be creating and dreaming a whole new world into being.

So, create through your uncertainty. Write your way through your process. Sing through your agony and your confusion. Fall and winter must come.

**Reach out to the hearts of others
through sharing your soul's song.**

△

WE CAME HERE
TO SING

We're living in a time when consciousness is changing at a rapid rate. Mistruths are being unearthed every moment of every day. The unsustainable towers of times past are falling to our feet. And so they should. For the artists, the writers, the leaders, the teachers, the poets, and the creators it can feel like a scary time to create. But we must create. For the polar opposite of creating is consuming, and overconsumption is the last thing the world needs right now.

Creativity is part of your true nature. It's a fundamental part of being human. And in times of uncertainty and confusion, creativity can help us find our way. In times of division and separation, creativity can bring connection. It's through creativity that we can mend what's been broken and weave a new future for our world.

Perhaps you're being called to surrender to a creative project that you'll share with others. Or perhaps you're being called to weave beauty in your home or in the way you cook. Maybe you're here to grow a garden. Or perhaps the seeds planted within you are calling you to find a new way of creating a sustainable Earth. Sing, sing, regardless, sing.

I know it can be bewildering to put your voice, your art, your creations, into the world when it feels like the unwinding and unbinding will never end. But if you're here to create, and your muse is whispering to you in the dead of night, then that's what you must do. Each of us has a note to sing in the orchestra of

Life. And when each of us shares this unique note, this frequency activates something deep within someone else. We were never meant to compete, we were never meant to compare – we came here to sing.

STARSEED ACTIVATION

'I'm ready to seed what I came here to share.

May I be sung. May I be sung. May I be sung.'

The Star Gardener

Don't lose yourself in the sky,
or get stuck in the Earth.

You are a weaver of worlds.
A heavenly dancer.

Planting Seeds with every step.

A bridge between spirit and matter.
The Star Gardener.
Here to help us remember.

△
THERE ARE CREATIONS SEEDED WITHIN YOU

There are creations seeded within you – planted before your birth. There are unborn possibilities yearning to be woven and creative solutions waiting to be realized. Songs of the ancient Earth singing to you to be once again sung, and new consciousness that's longing to be watered and breathed into life.

Surrender to the creations seeded within you, known and unknown. Perhaps they're beckoning you to, in some small way, reweave the web of Life. To stitch the soul in a little more. We came bearing keys for each other, and as you share your song it unlocks something in someone else.

Creativity and intuition come from the same sacred place; they can't be reproduced. They occur when we find ourselves flowing with the rest of Life – when we let our vessels merge with the other worlds and something that we didn't know was there is ushered in.

Earth is renowned as a planet of manifestation and creativity and yet so many of us have forgotten how to truly create. So much of humanity has been raised to consume – so focused on more more more that we've forgotten how to grow sustainably. Our consumption is killing us.

Trust the seeds that have been planted within you. Somewhere along the way we stopped seeing ourselves as artists, as creatives, as poets, as singers…. Yet to be human is to be creative.

It doesn't matter what the end result may be, just carve out time to express your soul through your creativity. Don't distract yourself with the pesky details of the outcome; rather, invite your creative soul to step forward and lead. The seeds planted within you will show you the way. They have intelligence within them, and all you need to do is tend to them through daily grounded, creative action.

Surrender to what scares and excites you. Lose yourself in what makes you come alive. Create with no attachment to the outcome. Find a way to weave beauty back into everyday life. For where there's creativity, Life and soul are present. And the world needs more of that now than ever.

SOUL INQUIRY

What does your soul most yearn to create?

What do you want to create just for the joy of it?

△
TRUST THE TIMING
OF YOUR LIFE

When you came here for a reason. When you came here for the possible chance of influencing the outcome. When you're living in a time when the future of the entire planet is uncertain, it's normal to feel as if time's running out. To mistrust the timing of your life and feel like you need to do things faster than your body allows. To go into overdrive.

It's when you feel like this that you simply must trust the limitations of your body and the timing of your life. There's a difference between rushing and urgency, and we're living in urgent times. We need to find a way to live sustainably, both for our bodies and the planet. Trusting the wave you came in on has never been more important than it is now.

We came to this world in waves. Waves of souls, each with their own unique role to play. Carried by cosmic tides, rolling in and out, in and out, in and out, in and out. Don't try to ride a wave that's not yours.

You didn't come here alone. It's not your sole responsibility to save the world. It's not even the responsibility of the wave. The cosmic tides are guided by an intelligent force. So don't take your mission to be the only mission.

Trust the wave you came in on.
Trust the timing of your life.

It's impossible to be always on, to be in full bloom all year round. This is the way of living that got us in this situation in the first place.

When it's your time to create, create. When it's your time to step forward and lead, step forward and lead. When it's your time to bloom, bloom. When it's your time to rest, rest. When it's your time to learn, learn. When it's your time to be led, be led, be led, be led.

When you trust the timing of your life you clear the way for the next wave to roll in. You allow the cosmic tide to do what it knows how to do. Resist the urge and the external pressure to be always on and to live like you have to grow grow grow, do do do, fight fight fight. The survival of the planet depends on our discernment.

If you trust the timing of your life enough to wait when it's time to wait, to go in when it's time to go in, then by the time the ocean clears you'll have something left to give – enough energy to paddle your way onto the wave that's meant for you.

So often, those who feel like they're here for a reason sense that time's running out, and they spend their life worrying that they might miss their moment. But the only way to miss your life or your moment is to spend your time worrying about missing it. To make decisions from the space of being afraid of missing out.

The tides of your life are magnificently orchestrated to come in and out in perfect unison. Don't race ahead and ride a wave that was never meant for you. You'll waste your precious time and energy and be no good to anyone or the world. Everything has a season and you're being called to trust the one you're in.

Don't let impatience, comparison, competition, pressure, or paranoia disturb the seeds that need watering. Trust that they know exactly what to do and when to do it. Which means you do too.

It seems that everyone has anxiety these days, and we're constantly scanning for something we might have missed or a possible threat. Keeping our mind and body pointed in the same direction as our soul is near impossible at such reactive speeds. Now, more than ever, we must remember with urgency to take a moment and trust the wave we came in on. To trust the wisdom of the seed. And to remember that we are the seeds.

SOUL INQUIRY

How can you trust the timing of your life a little bit more?

△
THIS, THIS, WE CAME
HERE FOR THIS

I know it can sometimes feel as though being alive at this time is too difficult or too chaotic or too volatile or harsh. And I know how easy it is to want to hide away – to avoid, to take cover, to disassociate, and escape it all.

These times, these chaotic, volatile times; these days of reckoning, of crumbling, of dismantling, of undoing. Perhaps we came here for this.

These times that haven't occurred before – perhaps these times are the very ones you chose to be here for. Perhaps you're not alone in your questioning and your yearning to resist them. Perhaps the very process of embracing them will be the gateway to your own healing and growth and contribute to the healing and growth of the collective.

**Perhaps you, we, all of us are actually the
cells of the Universe organizing itself. Perhaps
you, we, all of us are actually the imaginal
cells of the Universe rebirthing itself.**

Perhaps the resistance is really the fear of us changing form – going into the unknown chrysalis of our becoming. Perhaps the seeming chaos isn't chaos at all. Perhaps the chaos is all part of the plan. Perhaps the chaos is re-constelling us, both personally and collectively, so that together we can enter a whole new possible stage of humanity. Perhaps this, this, this, is the whole reason we came.

These times aren't pretty. But the awakening process never is. And make no mistake – we're all together waking up. Waking up individually and collectively. Waking up is rarely easy. It can feel like being startled from our peace, and all that we once relied on is becoming undone. I know this isn't comfortable, but growth rarely is. May we grow together through this.

If you find yourself in conflict, in upheaval, in crumbling (and of course we all will), do whatever you can to find your soul's center. Go to the very seed of your soul and plant yourself there. Lead from there. Weave your entire life from there.

If you find yourself in conflict, in upheaval, in crumbling, find your physical center. Go to the Earth. Plant yourself there. We're here to reweave the soul into everyday life; to seed the soul into the Earth. Not only to be spiritual and human, but to weave, fuse, merge, integrate the two. To become the Divine human. To prepare for the Children of the Sun. To become the golden ones. But alchemy cannot happen without first enduring the darkest of nights and walking through the fire.

Never before have we personally or collectively had access to all of the tools that we have today. All of the great secrets of the world's traditions have been freed from the libraries and are within our reach. All of the wisdom of the world's mystics and poets, the great teachers and beings of all of humanity can be read and found. We have access to it all at this pressing time. I know it can feel difficult and destabilizing to be living through times of change such as these, but I know, and I have a feeling that you do too, that this, this, perhaps we came here for this.

△

STAYING OPEN WHEN YOU MOST WANT TO CLOSE

The challenge of Life is to keep your heart open when you most want to close it. To let life crack you open again and again and again. To open through hurt and loss, disappointment, betrayal, and pain. To allow what's falling away to fall away.

Being human is a courageous act, and a life well lived is full of losses and tragedies, as well as triumphs and adventures. Holding the poles of Life is no easy feat, but make no mistake, this is a planet of polarity.

Wherever you find yourself at the moment, Life is coaxing you to keep your heart open, no matter how much it hurts. To find a way to unfold through the extremes. Perhaps you're going through a difficult time right now. Perhaps Life is testing you more than you think you can bear. Perhaps more than anything, you want to shut down and cut off. The grief is real. Personal and collective. The healing is going to take as long as it takes.

And while it feels personal, maybe it's not only personal. Perhaps our part is a thread in the great tapestry of the ages. Perhaps this invitation to open your heart is an invitation for us all to open the heart of humanity. Perhaps we can find comfort in that.

So go fiercely and also go gently. Treat yourself with the tenderness of a precious child because you are one. Take yourself into your own heart. One day, not too long from today, you'll look back at these times and be blown away at how far you and we all have come. If you're to do just one thing, do anything you can to keep your heart open. To open through the extremes.

SOUL INQUIRY

How can you keep your heart open?

△
WHEN YOU REALIZE THAT YOU ARE THE LEADER

I know how much courage it takes to tirelessly pave a path unpaved. I know how bewildering it can feel when, after waiting for someone to save you and lead you, you come to the sinking realization that the person might actually have to be you.

Gulp.

Being a leader in normal times is big in itself, but being a leader in times of change is a whole huge other thing to navigate. And these are changing times.

If you're being called forth, know that you're not alone. Trust the seed that's been planted within you. It knows the way. Be silently led by it. I know that when the ground is constantly changing it can feel scary and unsettling to step forth and pave a path uncertain. I also know that if something within is calling you forth, then that's what you must do. I've tried too many times to push down the call from within, and I've seen too many times what happens to a life when we do just that.

What I've come to know is that when we do ignore the call from within we also push down the Life force within and deny who we truly are. The more we ignore the Life force within and deny our true nature, the further away and unaligned from Life we get. And the longer we ignore the seed of the call within, the harder and harder it becomes to quieten. The more time that passes, the more substances, survival mechanisms, and ways of being we need to recruit to squash it.

If you came here to lead then that's what you must do.

SOUL INQUIRY

How are you being called to lead?

△
BECOMING GOLDEN

Your soul holds ancient codes, but these ancient codes can't be seeded if all of you is not here. Seed what you came here to seed. Sing the note that you came here to sing. Call your soul all the way in.

We're living in times of destruction and deconstruction. I know it's difficult; I know that in times like these it's easier to just go and run for cover, to wait it out, to feel like you'd rather be in the cave, to escape and gather those you know and be away from the rest of the world.

But this is not the life to be in the cave.
This is not the life to stay hidden away.
This is not the life to avoid anything.

The great reorganization is happening. It's going to be uncomfortable, but you're not the only one who's uncomfortable. You're not alone in this. You're not the only one who is fearful or who would prefer to stay underground until the great cosmic showers pass. And they will pass. Maybe not in your lifetime, but they will pass. We came here to play our part in this great cosmic show.

There will come a day when those to come will sing your name. Where the golden ones will praise you for being a birther, for being an alchemist, for clearing the way for them. For facing the dark and the uncomfortable so the engoldening can begin. And you'll take your place as one of the ancestral alchemists. Be the alchemist. Be the one who walks through the fire once more.

STARSEED ACTIVATION

'I surrender to my role as an alchemist.

I lean into the uncomfortable and open my heart when I most want to close.

I heal what I'm here to heal.

I face what I'm here to face.

I embrace what I'm here to embrace.

I take my place as an ancestor of times to come.

I welcome the shadows in order to transform past wounds into gold.

I embrace the seasons of my life

I commit to being here in matter.

I call my soul all the way in.

From my fingertips to my toes.'

PLANT YOURSELF HERE

How to Feel More at Home on Earth

△
THE CHALLENGE OF
BEING HUMAN

Being a soul is easy. It's being a human that's hard.

Being a soul having a human experience can sometimes be lonely, confusing, and painful. But at the same time, it can be incredibly glorious, magnificent, breathtaking, and sweet. The polarity and separation here on Earth is a lot for many to deal with, perhaps because they remember and long for the constant oneness of Source.

It's a miracle if we get through life with an open heart, front and back. But nature is miraculous and you're part of nature, so if you trust your own true nature and stay aligned to that, it's possible to live through the extremes of this human life with an open heart. This doesn't mean we become immune to the heartache and heartbreak of this world. Actually, the opposite is true – the greatest challenge in this life and all the others is to find a way to keep your heart open through the extremes.

If you find a way to keep your heart open through the heartache and heartbreak of being human then you'll also be able to welcome and be open to receiving the other extremes of being human – the joy, the love, and the bliss. You signed up for these extremes – they are part of Life on Earth. The birth and blossoming of spring and summer and the falling away and void of autumn and winter. We've learned to value only spring and summer, and the young over the old, and the birth over the death – but each is just as holy and each is necessary for us to fully experience what it is to be human.

Those who have allowed themselves to experience the inner autumns and winters are the ones who truly embody their humanity and can hold space for those who are going through their own versions of that. And we're all constantly being invited to do that. The more we allow our own inner autumns and winters, the more compassionate we can be to our fellow companions, and the more we see each other with tender care. We're suddenly capable of recognizing the great courage it takes to truly live this human journey with an open heart.

Indeed, it's the extremes of Life that initiate us the most. Through staying open to these extremes, we're able to experience Life fully, which I believe is the whole reason we chose to be here. Death gives way to birth, grief gives way to healing, separation gives way to union, resentment gives way to forgiveness – on and on it goes.

Like the buds blooming with wild abandon and then fearlessly throwing all they once were to the Earth's floor, surrendering to the fertile void so that come spring, they can continue to embrace this beautiful world.

When we zoom out and realize that we're each but a speck of exploded stardust in a Universe within a multiverse much greater than anyone in history could possibly fathom, it's almost impossible not to gain a greater perspective. If we were able to zoom out enough to see it, we'd realize the breathtaking beauty of this planet that so much of humanity has taken for granted.

The answer isn't to transcend and ignore the devastation that's happening here. The answer is also not to ignore the interconnectedness of it all. Just as we can't heal what we don't acknowledge in our own life, the same goes for us as a planet. I trust in nature's ability to regenerate. I believe that this planet can do that too, and we can do that too – but it'll require us to stop seeing ourselves as separate from nature.

**We must wake up and realize that
we *are* nature, and return to the Earth.**

And so anything we can do to support nature or our own nature – through trusting the seasons, through not pushing ourselves to grow grow grow, through connecting with the Earth itself, through protecting the most vulnerable – is necessary right now. We can hold the frequency of oneness and also acknowledge what's been severed. We can appreciate the world's ancient traditions while still acknowledging the brutal persecution that's occurred. We can be grateful for the blessings that we live with while supporting those who go without.

Each of us can be, if we allow it, part of nature's great regeneration. Each of us can be, if we allow it, part of the reweaving of the fabric of Life here on planet Earth. The garden is waiting for us to return to it. We were never kicked out in the first place. So let the trees be your cathedrals, the flowers your prayer books. May we return to the Earth, to the Earth, to the Earth.

The challenge for all souls having a human experience is to commit to being in the world. To having their soul fully embody their body, and to land all the way in, right down to the cells. Many Starseeds have a tendency toward transcendence over immanence; to transcend means to go beyond the here and now – to focus on the heavens and what's superior or supernatural over the reality of what's here, what's immanent, the matter of things.

If you have a natural leaning toward the heavens, then working on embodiment and with matter is likely what's needed. If you have a natural leaning toward the physical, then stretching yourself to the mystical and unity of Source is where to stretch to.

Those who lean completely toward immanence deny the soul and spirit of Life, focusing more on the physical reality of what's in the practical here and now. People who lean toward transcendence tend to lean toward transcending it all. Transcendence alone can lead to disassociation and bypassing our own and others' humanity and the reality of life. Immanence alone can lead to dismissing the connectedness of Life. We're being encouraged to find our way to hold both now.

If you find that you lean to one more than the other the challenge is to work on integrating the other so that the dance between heaven and Earth, masculine and feminine, spirit and matter can begin. So, if you've a tendency toward transcendence, how can you also hold the opposite of that and truly see what's happening at the other end of the spectrum of reality? If you've a tendency toward immanence, how can you raise your gaze to see the mystery that's woven through it all?

Most Starseeds are more comfortable with the angels and the heavens. They long for unity and oneness in a way that's so palpable it hurts. However, true oneness and unity is not and will not be possible until it's integrated for all on Earth. Right down to the cells of our body and all beings on this planet. It must be truly anchored here on Earth rather than being a concept that we escape to and hold in our consciousness. As above, so below. Heaven and Earth.

The purpose is not transcendence – it is integration. The soul is here on the Earth to perfect itself and experience itself. It's not perfect in itself and gracing the human experience with its presence. No.

The soul needs the human experience, just as the human experience needs the soul. Heaven needs the Earth just as the Earth needs heaven.

The soul is working on above and below at the same time. Cosmic and Earth. As above, so below. We chose to be here. It's time to commit to being fully, utterly, completely, and wholeheartedly here now.

STARSEED ACTIVATION

'I will not look away from what I don't want to see.

I choose to commit fully to being here now.'

SOUL INQUIRY

How can you commit more fully to being here now?

How can you embrace your humanity and the human experience more now?

△

Incarnation

It's easy to get sidetracked and move our gaze to the stars.
To long for a familiar, comfortable place – anywhere other than here.
To yearn for the infinite bliss of the union in the heavens
or the corner of the Universe in which you feel most comfortable.
You chose to be here now, so be here now.

Many souls struggle with the polarity of this human life.
The agony of the extremes that is being human. The grief, the death,
the endings, the conflict, the winter… the other side of where we long to
be, the family we were born into and the experiences we long to have.
But Life on Earth doesn't work like that.
You chose to be here now, so be here now.

We resonate with titles like empath and highly sensitive
and try to hide ourselves away from the harshness of the world.
Our hearts are broken by the brokenness of an unsustainable world,
and so it's much easier if we turn our gaze someplace else
to ease the pain of a world such as this.
You chose to be here now, so be here now.

This time in which we're living is uncomfortable, there's no doubt.
Our hearts should be broken. Our systems should be crumbling.
Our old ways of being should be questioned.
Our curriculum is right in front of us.
You chose to be here now, so be here now.

△
THE ORIGINAL SEVERING

We live in a time when many of us have become disconnected from the land beneath us. Somewhere along the way a severing occurred. A moment when it became too painful to stay connected. Since then many of us have been disconnected from the Earth, unable to feel at home, and as such we find ourselves wondering where we truly belong.

Wandering around not feeling held. Supported. At home. Shape-shifting our way through lives, cities, friends, and experiences, and looking to others to fill the void of the holding and belonging of what the Earth once gave us. Taking. Clutching. Conquering. Longing for others to receive us fully as the Mother once did. Clueless to the truth that she's still there, waiting for us to remember, and for that part in us that's so longing to receive Her embrace to awaken once more.

When you consciously connect with the Earth a veil is lifted and the Earth opens up and receives you more fully. You're able to be held fully. Stagnant energy falls away as you remember that you're connected to all the things on the planet. When you connect with the electromagnetic pulse of the Earth, each of your cells comes more alive.

As you connect with the Earth and honor the keepers of it – those who came before you – the land opens up more fully and those ancestors don't just become guardians of the land, but guardians of you too.

When you consciously connect with the Earth a veil is lifted and it opens up and receives you more fully. You're able to be held fully, drink from Her sweet waters, and exhale with the wind what no longer serves. Stagnant energy falls away and you become connected to all things on the planet. When you properly connect you activate the electromagnetic pulse and something begins to flow and come alive, and as it does, each of your cells comes more alive too.

STARSEED ACTIVATION

'I allow myself to connect to the Earth.

To return to the arms of the Mother.

To allow this planet to be my home for now.

I surrender and allow myself to be truly held.'

△

Plant Yourself Here

Invite your soul to come all of the way in.
From your knees to your nose, your cheeks to your toes.

Fully embody your life.
Drop the defensive walls.
Let your soul land and occupy each and every single cell.

Anchor all parts of you into the here and now.
Life is here even when death is here.

Birth isn't possible without it.
And you came here to birth this world anew.
Don't you remember?

Fully commit to living this life.
Put your two feet and your ancient soul
wholly and completely in.

Plant yourself here.

△
YOU'RE SPECIAL AND
ALSO NOT SPECIAL

You're extraordinary and also ordinary in your extraordinariness. You're special and also not special in your specialness. You're unique and also not unique in your uniqueness. Life on Earth is filled with exquisite miracles. And these exquisite miracles are also ordinary. All of Life is that.

Just watch someone being born or dying. These are both the most extraordinary and ordinary things at the very same time. Grief is like that too. So personally excruciating and yet also the most normal response to the side effects of living a life on Earth. If you let yourself fully live you can't sidestep it.

The true nature of nature is nothing short of miraculous. You are nature and so you are miraculous too. The same intelligence that tells the daffodil when to bloom is within each of your cells too. Remember that, surrender to that. Don't get in the way of trying to control the intelligence of who you are through comparison or doubt. Trust that as the hawthorn knows how to turn flowers into fruit, if you allow it you'll conspire with Life to create yours too. And while you're at it, give the gift of trusting in the miraculous true nature of others, too.

Don't judge your emotions or attempt to control them. Let your feelings flow like the weather. Emotions are feelings in motion – if we let them flow and choose to focus them in a beneficial way, miracles can occur.

We're moving out of an era of individualism and into one of true togetherness. But in order to truly come together we must acknowledge our differences. We must see how special and unique we are while also seeing the same uniqueness in others. To acknowledge that we've not been seeing that in others. To stop our divisive ways by first acknowledging that we've been part of the division, whether consciously or unconsciously.

We've been taught that there isn't enough room for everyone and that therefore we need to compete with one another. But flowers don't compete with each other – the cherry blossom doesn't think it's any more or less special than the rose – they embrace all that they are and bloom alongside each other as if it's the most extraordinary and ordinary thing in the world. Because it is and they are. And you are too.

SOUL INQUIRY

How can you surrender to the unique miraculous true nature of who you are?

How can you surrender to the unique miraculous true nature of other people?

△
FIND YOUR FLOWER

I believe that nature is teaching us how to be human every moment of every day, and that flowers in particular hold information about who we are and who we're becoming, blooming, and transforming into.

I believe that here on this planet we each have a flower that holds a similar quality to who we are at a soul level. Celestial notes to self. Flowers sent from the soul to ourselves on the Earth to remind us who we really are.

I believe that in different periods of our life, as new things are blooming within us, the qualities that are wanting to open up within us can be coaxed out by working with flowers.

I believe that it's impossible to work with flowers and not have your heart opened more and more, and little by little, they will return you to the true nature of who you really are.

SOUL INQUIRY

If you were a flower, what flower would you be?

△

We Are Like Flowers

Maybe flowers are here to teach us how to be human.
How to unashamedly embrace our true nature,
no matter how different or beautiful.

To realize that we're not meant to look or sound or act the same.
That diversity isn't just important but necessary for Life. To keep
remembering that there's a sacred timing to things, that there's enough
room for everyone, and that it's impossible to bloom all year round.

Maybe flowers are here to teach us how to be human. To stand
tall like the poppy and strong like the thistle. To be resilient,
like heather, and reach our roots deep like the fig. To defy the
norm, like the hawthorn. To courageously open through our
fears wholeheartedly, like the peony. To be unapologetic, like the
passionflower. To remember our sweet innocence, like jasmine.

To take a leap and go first, like the daffodil. To be willing to risk it
all, like cherry blossom. To know it's never too late, like the winter
rose. To trust the changing seasons of our life, like the hydrangea.

Some of us are here to inspire, like the garden rose. Others are here
to activate and protect, like the crown of thorns. Some are sensitive,
like the orchid. Others are here to leave a mark, like the lily.

Yes, perhaps that's what flowers are here to teach us:
How to be our unique selves on planet Earth.

△

THE AWAKENING PROCESS
AND THE IMPORTANCE
OF INTEGRATION

The awakening process never ends. When we experience our first awakening, it can feel as though we're remembering all of the secrets of the Universe. But after we come back down to Earth for an integrated breath we realize that the awakening process is a lifelong process, and that we're forever remembering and feeling into the great mystery of being a soul having a human experience.

Falling in love is like that too, and so is having really good sex. The first time it happens we're sure that we've found some secret code. An answer. Arrived in some end place. But Life is forever changing and it never stops unfolding for us. This is the great spiral of the human life.

I've had many awakening experiences. Some have been spontaneous, while others have been more gradual and drawn out. Some have been extremely physical, while others have been more subtle and internal. Some have been ecstatic and blissful, some absolutely excruciating; most have been both. Some have given me answers and others have given me questions to live into, unearthing more and more questions. The further I get into the seasons of my life, the more certain I am of the mystery itself. It's true what they say – the more we know, the less we know with certainty.

Perhaps you're going through a period of spontaneous awakening – receiving visions and having experiences that are out of the ordinary.

In the West, little is known about the process of spontaneous awakening, and it can feel very scary when we're going through it alone. Elsewhere in the world, these can be seen as auspicious experiences, and those going through them are treated with tender care – like laboring women or babies in the birth canal. The more awakenings I experience the more similar to birth I see the process.

Many people glamorize the awakening process; however, in reality it's much messier and more difficult than most of us believe. We must first let go of what we think we know for sure and how we make sense of the world. This isn't easy. The awakening process (even when it's 'spontaneous') takes a considerable amount of time to integrate, and awakening without integration can leave us feeling very ungrounded and unstable.

May we all live into our awakenings so we can truly seed what we came here to share. Without integration, the seeds can't live on without us. There's nothing to contain them, to hold them, to nourish them. May the seeds live on long after we've gone. There are new souls coming who are calling for us to prepare the soil for them. Can you feel them? They are near.

It's no secret that we're going through a global awakening right now. Even some of those who have long been asleep are beginning to stir. Much of what we once believed was certain is crumbling; everything inauthentic or unaligned or unsustainable is falling to our feet. Ways of being that we once relied upon are no longer working. Life as we knew it isn't just changing – it's forever changed.

The planets have begun their sacred dance.

We're living through a time that's been predicted by medicine men and women through the ages. Be mindful of those who paved the way for you – those who painstakingly prepared the bed so you could wake up from your slumber more easily than they did. And if you've been the one who's painstakingly made the bed, try to remember that those who are just waking up were asleep, unaware of all that you did. Give it and them time. They will come around.

If you're in the midst of an awakening (the process never ends), treat this time as deeply sacred and give yourself ample space to ground and integrate the extreme changes you're going through. Treat yourself with gentle care and give yourself plenty of time to integrate and rest – no matter how spontaneous. Water your precious seeds and let them take root.

Trust which seeds are for the world and which are just for you. Sometimes precious jewels need time to land and be cradled in your hands before they can be passed around. The deeper your roots, the deeper the impact you'll have. Trust the timing of your life.

STARSEED ACTIVATION

'I allow myself to surrender to the awakening process that's right for me.

I take things slowly and integrate my experiences each and every day.

I trust the timing of my life.'

The One True Authority

If you put someone on a pedestal
or allow them more authority over you,
you'll eventually need to
cut

them

down

in order to stand   at the same level.

You can avoid all of this by not giving another person or system
or external force the authority over you in the first place.

When you voice the truth, your truth,
it can be felt by all those around.
It doesn't mean it's THE truth or the truth
of all involved, but it's your truth.

When you voice this truth with an open heart,
it makes it easier for someone else to access theirs.
And that clears the path for a mutual truth
to be reached, realized, and found.

Things are not only black and white. One thing or the other.
No one knows what's true for you more than you.

The one true authority of your soul has only ever been You.

△
YOU WILL NOT BE LIKED

Do not waste this precious life trying to fit in. It will never work and it will be a waste of a life. Yours. Who you are is far more than you could even begin to fathom. You were never meant to fit in. Being you is the whole point.

Try to control and please all of those around you. Bend and shapeshift, and by all means squeeze yourself into that invisible box. You will not be liked, and that's okay.

It doesn't matter what you do or how much you attempt to avoid it, your presence is designed by default to trigger something in someone else. To bubble up to the conscious what they might prefer not to see. You will not be liked, and that's okay.

Through no fault of your own, your being on this planet will make someone feel uncomfortable. You may as well be comfortable yourself while it happens. And it will happen. You will not be liked, and that's okay.

At some stage, and perhaps at many stages, you'll be the cause of someone else's sadness, undoing, or rage. Your very existence will remind them of something that they might prefer not to see. You'll be cursed and cut off because of who you are. And it'll have nothing to do with you.

You will not be liked, and that's okay.

△

BEING COMFORTABLE WITH BEING UNCOMFORTABLE

As humans we are cyclic beings, like the rest of nature. As cyclic beings we're not meant to stay the same. Change is scary. It's uncomfortable. And the challenge is to learn to be comfortable with being uncomfortable.

Many of us would prefer to avoid the uncomfortable. But to avoid the uncomfortable is to avoid growth, and to avoid growth is to avoid our own true nature. And if we avoid our true nature we'll fall out of flow with life. Things get stuck in our life and our body. We must endeavor to learn to get comfortable in the uncomfortable.

By leaning in to conflict with an open heart, growth can come. The trick is to stay in it, not to fight, flee, or freeze. To breathe through it; to commit to being in the uncomfortable and find a way to open your heart; to have love and expansion as the final destination. I've had to learn each and every day to get more comfortable in the uncomfortable.

I grew up not being comfortable in uncomfortable conversations or situations. Avoiding conflict above all else. When conflict hit I froze, shut down, and did everything I could to get out of the uncomfortableness. I'd learned to be scared of being in the uncomfortableness of conflict or disharmony. But what I've discovered is that often the uncomfortableness we experience in relationships is actually an invitation for transformation. A possible opportunity for growth in both people and a deepening into love and expansion.

It may result in a new, deeper, more fulfilling chapter in the relationship or it may result in a healthy ending, creating space for the destined new. But it does generally require two willing parties who want to be transformed through it. And in order to be transformed through it we must find a way to move through the fight, flight, freeze response. To breathe through it and keep our hearts open through it. Otherwise we'll continue to repeat the same thing over and over again, and find ourselves circling around and around and around. Or we'll simply avoid fully living life, and when we do that, part of us dies.

Invite all parts of you to be present. Learn to be comfortable with being uncomfortable. It's how we grow together.

SOUL INQUIRY

How comfortable are you with being uncomfortable?

When you get uncomfortable do you fight, flee, or freeze?

Only You Know What's True for You

When you put the opinions of others
above what you know to be true.

When you make the mistake of taking your
pulse from someone else's feelings.

When you catch yourself beginning to believe
what strangers say about you.

When you let the energy of the external
world question your innocence.

When you feel yourself absorbing others' unfelt
emotions and mistaking them for your own.

Say: I am not that. That's not who I am.

△
IT'S NONE OF YOUR BUSINESS

It's none of your business what anyone else believes, especially if they believe in something different from you. Don't take it upon yourself to control what they should say or do or think. Instead, trust them to find their own way and let it be a way different from yours.

We're multifaceted souls in multifaceted ancestral bodies, so you can't possibly know what it's like to embody their cells, just as they can never know what it's like to embody yours. You have your karma to burn and path to walk. They have theirs too. Don't make the mistake of thinking that what you see on the surface is what it's like beneath the water. That what's happening on the outside reflects what's happening on the inside. Everyone is fighting their own complex battles. Journeying through all kinds of circumstances, conditioning, patterns, inner seasons, and cosmic weather. Different to you and also just like you.

This life is a great initiation for the soul, and getting through it with an open heart is a triumph. Do your best to keep your heart open and don't throw intentional daggers that might make it easier for someone else to close theirs.

Once we're done with this Life it's likely we'll remember that we're not doing this thing called Life alone. But we're each playing our part in the great orchestra of Life. You're not the conductor, so do whatever you can to focus on playing your instrument and trust others to play theirs too.

△
YOUR SACRED VESSEL

Treasure your body each and every day. Don't take it for granted. It's the best companion you'll ever have. Treat it with love, kindness, and respect. Feed it, water it, honor it, adore it, cherish it. It's the whole reason you're here.

I know that being a soul in a body can sometimes feel difficult. That sometimes it doesn't move or work as you wish it would. Or go quite fast enough. If I were to wish one thing for us it would be that we'd not waste one more day without acknowledging all that it does. Our precious, precious body – more valuable than all of the treasures in the world.

Let's go back to when we were children. To the wonder of tasting and seeing and hearing for the first time. To the textures, the sounds, the lights, and the faces. Yes, this body is your companion for life. A loyal friend who agreed to be with you through this magnificent, crazy, bumpy, beautiful, messy, sometimes extremely difficult experience called being human.

Without your body, you don't exist here. Your body is the thing that makes it all possible.

Perhaps our body's faults, limitations, so-called shortcomings, aches and pains, bad digestion, that bung knee, the epic period pain are not things that slow down our human experience. Perhaps they're actually ensuring we can fully participate in this human experience and do what we came here to do. So we can feel what we came here to feel. Learn what we came here to learn. Share what we came here to share. Heal what we came here to heal. Create what we came here to create. Seed what we came here to seed.

If we believe we're souls here having a human experience then we must worship the body. For nothing is possible without it. This seems so obvious, but it's a huge one for those who may have a tendency to transcend rather than embody.

So, the next time you complain that your body's holding you back, ponder this thought: Perhaps your body isn't holding you back – perhaps it's what's holding you through it. Making possible that very thing you're feeling held back from. Holding you every moment of every day. The ultimate companion.

SOUL INQUIRY

What is your body yearning for?

△
YOUR BODY IS INTUITIVE

Intuition isn't a fluffy, lightweight thing – it's much more grounded than that and is communicated through the physical body. We're all intuitive and it's through our physical senses that we receive our intuition. My body, your body, our bodies are intuitive. Without them, we're not intuitive at all. Your clairvoyance is your body. Your clairsentience is your body. Your claircognizance is your body. Your clairaudience is your body.

The more grounded and incarnated our soul is in our body, the more we're able to discern our intuitive senses. When I was in my twenties, my intuitive teacher Sonia Choquette taught me that intuition is pointless unless you act on it; and my creative mentors drilled this same teaching into me when it came to ideas and creativity (which I believe come from the same place as intuition).

The more you work with your intuition and your body, the more heightened each of these senses will become. The more grounded in your body you get, the further your light can reach and the clearer your intuitive senses will become.

YOUR PRIMARY INTUITIVE SENSES

For those who are new to the intuitive senses of the body, here is a brief overview of the main ones. In my experience we tend to have a primary intuitive sense, but it's also important to know that we have access to all of these senses and can work on strengthening every one.

Clairvoyance – clear seeing

This is the most common intuitive sense. Generally, our clairvoyance will manifest when we can see through our mind's eye or through visions. You don't have to physically see something in the flesh or real life to be clairvoyant. If clairvoyance is your primary intuitive sense, you'll probably use language such as 'I really see what you mean,' or 'I can really get a vision of where you're going with that.'

Clairaudience – clear hearing

Clairaudience is our ability to sense things through hearing. Again, this could be through actually hearing something in reality or it could be through listening to our inner ear. People who have a heightened clairaudient ability may find that they're hypersensitive when it comes to the sounds around them, and may need to spend a lot of time on their own or in a quiet place because their ears pick up everything.

When I'm doing my writing, I often walk in nature because I find the motion really helps. As I'm walking, it's as if I'm being led by my inner ear to hear the whispers of my soul.

Claircognizance – clear knowing

Claircognizance is the intuition that comes through a certain knowing. Creative concepts and ideas often come through claircognizance – one second previously there was no idea, the next second a whole concept has landed in your mind in full. You can't explain how you know it, you just do.

This sense can be one of the hardest to trust because it's easy to confuse it with your head as it's based on innate 'knowing.' The way to differentiate between the intuitive knowing and the logical knowing or thinking is that the former is more of an inner knowing and it often comes as a gentle yet deep whisper.

Clairsentience – clear feeling

The fourth main intuitive sense is clairsentience, which means clear feeling. This is a very common one for empaths, who are often able to pick up if there's just been an argument in the room or if there's been lots of laughter and joy around.

Clairsentients tend to be overly sensitive to other people's energies and need to spend a lot of time on their own to get grounded into their own physical energy body. As a clairsentient, things can get tricky if you're not aware of how your body absorbs and picks up information, because you can get confused as to whether you're picking up your own feelings or the feelings of other people.

Below are some of the lesser-known 'clair' senses:

Clairtangency – clear touching

Clairtangency people can receive information through their sense of touch. They may pick up textures or physical sensations when they receive their intuitive guidance.

Clairsalience – clear smelling

Clairsalience people are very in touch with their sense of smell. As with all of the clairs this doesn't need to be an actual physical smell – it can be an inner smell that they experience. Each smell delivers information; for example, lavender for a particular great aunt who loved her garden.

Clairgustance – clear tasting

Clairgustance people receive information through their sense of taste. As they're receiving their guidance, they can have a physical sensation in which they experience a particular flavor or a memory of a taste as a way of communicating information.

While we have access to all of these senses, in my experience people tend to have one or two senses that are the strongest, through which they first receive their information. After they receive their information through one of their senses they may then receive more information from other senses – almost as if the senses are communicating with each other or helping the individual to paint a fuller picture. For example, I often receive my intuitive information through clairaudience first. Once I receive the 'whisper' I then receive a feeling (clairsentience) and then a visual (clairvoyance).

SOUL INQUIRY

What do you think is your strongest intuitive sense?

△
THE GROUNDED EMPATH

The Oxford English Dictionary describes an empath as 'a person with the paranormal ability to perceive the mental or emotional state of another individual.' I agree with this definition, but I'd like to expand on it, as I believe that emotional energy can be stored in objects and places as well as in people; I call this the stored emotions of environment and object, and I believe they're imprinted by the people who come into contact with them. That's the emotional energy that can be stored in the place and object. I also believe that, compared to a non-empath, an empath experiences their own emotions and feelings at a heightened level.

I believe we all fit in somewhere on the empath spectrum), but for ease of understanding I'll describe those who are high on the spectrum as 'empaths' and those who are low as a 'non-empaths.'

Before I go on, it's important to say that we shouldn't use the title 'empath' as a way to 'other' ourselves (or others) from the world. Being an empath doesn't make us extra 'special' – we all exist on the continuum. In order to be a Grounded Empath it's crucial that we don't see ourselves as extra special or as a victim of the harsh energy or emotions of the world.

Being an empath can be a gift, provided the individual knows how to be responsible for it and uses it in an empowered way. In my personal experience, and also from working with thousands of people all around the world, many empaths aren't equipped with the understanding and tools required to manage, navigate, and use their gift in a way that allows them to thrive physically and emotionally.

In the last chapter we explored the different intuitive senses that we all have as humans, one of which is clairsentience, or 'clear feeling.' I believe that empaths have a high clairsentient ability in particular – compared to non-empaths – so it's the level of emotions that an empath is able to pick up on that makes them an empath.

Empaths have the ability to feel heightened emotional and mental states. This can be a seemingly positive thing – for example, when an empath meditates, has an excited conversation, or watches a joyful movie, they'll experience a heightened level of positive emotions compared to a non-empath.

However, this heightened level of input can also work in an apparently negative way. For example, if an empath is involved in an argument or enters a room in which an argument has just occurred, they could experience these 'negative' emotions more intensely, due to the level of input they might absorb through their clairsentience.

Another thing to consider is that the empath can pick up on the energy of a place or objects more readily than the non-empath. For example, if they visit a second-hand store some empaths may pick up on the energy of all of the objects owned by different people, and the emotions stored in them, whereas the non-empath will likely be unaware of such things.

Likewise, if an empath enters a sacred place with beautiful devotional energy, such as a temple, they can pick up on this harmonious energy more than a non-empath would. So being an empath isn't just about being more susceptible to funky energy – empaths are also more susceptible to harmonious energy.

Energetically, empaths are more open or porous. So, while the stimuli may be the same, what the empath experiences is amplified. For example, if an empath and a non-empath watch the same sunset, the non-empath will feel their own emotions, such as joy and optimism, while the empath will likely feel an amplified version of these emotions, such as extreme joy and extreme optimism. However, the empath doesn't only experience the physical setting of the Sun – they also experience the emotions, feelings, and energy of the place where they're watching it from, and these can be positive, negative, or anything in between. If the empath happens to be with other people, they'll also pick up on their emotions.

Empaths are especially sensitive to unfelt, unprocessed, and unclaimed emotions and mental activity. For example, if an empath is around people and places that are bypassing the emotions, they're more likely than a non-empath would be to pick up on these emotions and confuse them with their own if they don't have a way to distinguish between the two.

An empath experiences multiple stimuli in their everyday life, including everything that we interact with in the world, other people's expressed and unexpressed emotions and feelings, and the stored emotions of environment and object. While an empath experiences more stimuli, they also experience amplified emotions and feelings themselves. And so it's no surprise that an empath can experience emotional overload.

Using the analogy of a traditional letterbox, we can say that a non-empath has one letterbox in which they experience their emotions and feelings, whereas an empath has four – their own emotions and feelings (often at a heightened level), other people's conscious and subconscious emotions, the stored emotions from places, and the stored emotions from objects. So an empath is potentially receiving from four different inputs.

This is why it's crucial for an empath's well-being that they develop skills to manage the flow of input. Of course, as we're all multidimensional, we all exist somewhere on the empath spectrum. Many Starseeds identify as being highly empathic.

I believe that we can become an empath in three different ways. Some of us come into this life as a soul-level empath (already sensitive), while others' sensitivities are activated through their life experiences (often as a child, and often through a traumatic event) or through an awakening experience. If you resonate with being an empath, you may find that your empathic gifts have been activated more than once; for example, you may have been born as an empath and then your sensitivities were enhanced through a life experience or an awakening. I do believe that genetics play a role in this.

Soul-level empath: Some people come into this life as an empath, with a heightened ability to feel and understand the energy around them. This is a soul gift – something that's in their spiritual field as a small child. Some children who are born empathic are supported by parents or guardians who know how to manage this gift, but others are not. If a soul level empath is not taught how to manage their empathic nature as a child, then discovering tools to do this can be transformative.

Life-experience empath: Many people become empathic through experiencing some kind of trauma in life, often as a child. Their empathic reading skills could have been formed as a coping mechanism, a way to check that they're safe in the world. Behaviors such as hypervigilance – constantly scanning the energy around them to check they're okay – are an example of this.

Those who are empathic from a significant life experience are most likely to feel disempowered by their empathic abilities. They're likely to have learned to determine their safety or self-worth by reading the energy of others around them. They may also have a sense of being good or bad that's based on other people's opinions of them or the way they feel.

The invitation for the life experience empath is to learn to see their empathic ability as a strength that they're in control of, through finding tools to manage it in an empowered way. Whenever possible, it's helpful to seek professional support when processing past traumas, although I realize that not all life experience empaths will be able to do this.

Awakened empath: When we go through a significant awakening experience our senses can become heightened overnight and even after integration time our sensitivity can remain there. Someone can display or experience empathic traits through their awakening experiences and while these traits are at their most extreme during the awakening process, they can often remain afterward. For the awakened empath, it's necessary to have tools to manage this new empathic nature, in order to integrate their awakening and use these increased sensitivities as a helpful gift that serves them and others.

THE HIDDEN POWER OF THE EMPATH

An empath has the power to release, hold on to, increase, or shift the energy with their presence. That is, through coming into contact with other people, places, and objects, they have the potential to receive or transform the energy. There are many ways to do this. For example, if I'm having a difficult conversation with someone and want to consciously shift the energy, I'll imagine a rose between us and that all communication is flowing through the rose. I'm always astounded by the subtle shift this can make in transforming the energy of the conversation.

There are also physical ways to shift energy. One thing I do often is altar work, whether in my own home or when traveling to new places. Altar work is all about the intention you bring. You can use different sacred objects, such as candles, oracle cards, and fresh flowers; I also like using sacred smoke from dried plants in my garden. Other examples of actions you can take to shift your energy are exercise, dancing, writing in your journal, screaming into a pillow, decluttering, shaking, having a bath, or walking in nature.

Many empaths don't know this, and feel as though they're victims of the energy with which they come into contact. As a result, they often view the world around them as overly harsh. I believe that if more empaths knew that their sensitivity had the potential to be a real strength and a tool for transformation, the world would be a very different place.

As empaths, our sensitivity can be a powerful tool and gift, but if we don't know how to manage, work with, and take responsibility for this gift, we can become confused and suffer from low self-esteem, doubt, and overstimulation; this can affect our health and result in isolation. It can also stop us from fully embracing who we are and why we came here.

An empath has the power to receive and shift energy consciously – that is, their presence has the potential to bring about energetic shifts. However, if they don't know this, they'll find themselves unconsciously absorbing and resending the same frequency.

Because of their increased sensitivity, overstimulation and overwhelm can be more commonly experienced by empaths. This is why a regular practice of understanding what is ours, what is someone or someplace else's, and the active management of energy is really important. Most empaths haven't learned these tools from a young age and so in a bid to manage their energy input to avoid overwhelm, they run away or hide from the world because it's 'too harsh' and they feel like they're 'too much.'

Many empaths were raised by parents who didn't know how to support their sensitive children, and as a result, they've learned survival techniques and believe that they need to avoid certain situations, conversations, or topics because they don't have the strength to deal with such things without it taking them down energetically.

Many of the empaths I know relate to the scenario of arriving at a party, a concert, or a busy public place and then immediately locating the restroom and the exit, in case they need to escape. While spending time alone to recharge and clear out emotionally and energetically is crucial for an empath's well-being, this way alone of managing our energy and emotions can result in a loss of connection with others, and it can stop us from fully stepping into our soul mission.

I know this from my own experience. As a child I'd close myself off from my family and spend extended periods in my room at night because I'd reached an overload of emotional input and didn't know how to process it all. I didn't know that the reason I felt overloaded was that I'd absorbed others' unfelt emotions. I didn't know that I had a choice as to what I'd absorb, and I certainly didn't know that I could develop the power to shift the energy at will.

Later, I developed behaviors such as avoiding parties or public places because I didn't know how to manage the input of all of the emotions and feelings I had. Throughout my twenties I reached for alcohol and food as a way of managing this.

If we believe that we're victims of the energy around us, then when we experience emotions within or around us we're likely to perpetuate that energy, whether desirable or undesirable, without realizing that we have a choice.

It's important to be clear that transmuting energy is not bypassing it. Being an empath can be a wonderful gift, and it's also important that we integrate, ground, and take responsibility for living with this gift.

ON BECOMING THE GROUNDED EMPATH

The Grounded Empath is someone who sees their sensitivity as a gift and knows how to manage it. They see their empathic nature as a power, rather than something they're powerless over. They don't see themselves as a victim of the energy of the world and don't bypass what they see, feel, and experience.

A Grounded Empath knows that they can not only read the emotions, feelings, and energy around them, but they can choose to receive/absorb it, they can choose to cut off from it, or, and this is the real power – they can choose to shift it. The Grounded Empath knows that they can choose how they respond to and what they do with the energy around them. The Grounded Empath has the ability to transform emotions, energy, and feelings for themselves, on behalf of others and for the collective.

This is what I believe is the role of the empath in these times. But in order for the empath to do this, to become grounded, they first need to understand that their ability to absorb, process, or shift emotions and energy is a strength rather than a weakness or something in which they have no say (or are victim to).

A Grounded Empath knows that they can shift energy with their presence. They're in control of their sensitivity and see it as a powerful tool they can use. They know their place in the world, have learned how to transmute and alchemize energy, and take regular responsibility for their gift through daily grounded action.

Now more than ever we need empaths to be healthy, empowered, activated, and confident. Now more than ever we need empaths to claim their power of transmuting energy and being the alchemists of energy, emotions, and feelings. Now more than ever we need empaths to come out of hiding and work together to bring about genuine change through grounded action and active processing of what they pick up on.

Becoming a Grounded Empath takes time and practice. If the Grounded Empath exists at one end of a spectrum, at the other end would be the Ungrounded Empath.

Here are some descriptions of the two; see where you fit on the continuum between grounded and ungrounded with your empathic state of being.

Characteristics of the Grounded Empath

- Understands how to process the energy around them, so they know what's theirs and what isn't

- Knows how to manage their energy and likely has a daily practice to empty out on an energetic level

- Is able to take responsibility for their energetic well-being in an empowered way
- Is clear on boundaries and takes responsibility for their needs
- Knows that they get to choose when to absorb something energetically and when to shift it
- Knows that they're in control of their gift to feel and shift energy, and that they get to decide what to do with their energy
- Doesn't run away from or avoid the uncomfortable for fear of it taking them down. Knows how to be in the uncomfortable, to stay in their power, and to transform through it
- Actively decides what to absorb, what to cut off from, and what to transmute
- Doesn't gloss over or bypass difficult truths, conversations, or experiences
- Is open to healing from any traumatic events that have made them hypervigilant, codependent, or feeling like they're a victim of the energy of the world
- Has activated their inner mother and is able to practice genuine self-care
- Knows that they get to choose when to receive energy for alchemizing it, and receiving energy because they want to absorb it or merge with it
- Knows how to turn their feelings into action to avoid stagnation and overwhelm
- Actively uses tools such as nature, meditation, dance, exercise, and other forms of expression to avoid build-up or stagnation of energy

Characteristics of the Ungrounded Empath

- Thinks that they have no power over the energy with which they come into contact

- Doesn't know how to process the energy around them, or their own energy, and likely doesn't know what's theirs and what they've absorbed from the world around them or other people

- Becomes overwhelmed by all that they're feeling and believes that their only option is to remove themself from situations to avoid depletion

- Believes they're a victim of the harsh energies of the world

- Avoids conflict or uncomfortable situations at all costs

- Doesn't recognize that they have the power to decide whether or not to absorb or transform the energy around them

- Is often confused by their feelings and unsure which are theirs and which are other people's

- Is afraid of setting clear boundaries

- Finds themself in codependent relationships

- May be stuck in a flight, flight, freeze response

On the next page you'll find the Grounded Empath Tool, which will support you in identifying and sorting your empathic feelings and deciding what to do with them. This will help you process your feelings and the energies you pick up as you go through your day. I recommend doing this, or a process like this, on a regular basis.

SOUL INQUIRY

On the scale below, plot where you feel you fit currently:

Non-empath   Empath
(not highly sensitive)   (highly sensitive)

├──┤

*If you identify as being an empath, plot where you
feel you currently fit on the time line below.*

Grounded   Ungrounded
Empath   Empath

├──┤

*Are there any things that you're being called to do to claim
your sensitivity as a gift and become even more grounded?*

△
THE GROUNDED EMPATH TOOL

In a journal or a notebook, or directly on the page below, complete the following steps.

1. I'm feeling...

Write down all the feelings or energies you're currently experiencing. For example, *'I'm feeling nervous in my belly.'*

_____

_____

2. Who/what does it belong to?

Connect each feeling or energy you've listed in step one by drawing lines to the 'home' that best describes the source of the feeling or energy. For example, *'The nervousness in my belly is from my friend (someone else).'*

| Myself | Someone else (Who?) | Place | Object |

3. Decide what to do:

Decide what you want to do with the feeling or energy:

Release it   Shift it   Hold on to it   Deepen or increase it

4. Grounded action

Write down how you're going to respond to the feeling or energy. What grounded action are you going to take to either release it, shift it, hold on to it, deepen it, or increase it?

5. Action statement

Create a Grounded Empath Action Statement by combining your answers to the four previous steps using the template below. For example:

'I'm feeling: nervous in my belly from: the conversation I had with Terry this morning and I'm going to: release this feeling or energy by: writing in my journal and going for a run.'

I'm feeling *(your answer to step one)*:

from *(your answer to step two)*:

and I'm going to *(your answer to step three)*:

by *(your answer to step four)*:

△

Don't Run It through Your System

It's not helpful to run the energy of the world through your system.
It's not helpful to attempt to carry the weight of the world
on your back alone.

It's not helpful to let the problems of the world overwhelm you.
Action isn't possible from a place of overwhelm.
A life's work isn't possible if your way of being isn't sustainable.
Saving the world isn't your personal mission.

Start where you are.
Carry what's in front of you.
Be responsible for what's yours.

Do what you can do.
Show up, day after day after day.
Stay grounded, transmute what you can,
and be moved by daily action.

Be a revolutionary and rest hard and deep so you can
wake up and do it again and again and again.
This isn't a sprint.
You're needed for longer than that.

△
TRANSMUTING ENERGY INTO ACTION

Don't let the energy of these times cause you to flee or freeze or stagnate. This is the time for action. Action doesn't need to be reactionary doing. Rest can be action too. Staying home and baking bread can be revolutionary. Don't stay in the frequency of overwhelm. Find a way, big or small, not to be a victim of the energy around you. Use the energy. Let your mind and body be moved. Confuse the energy with movement. Ground it. Transmute it into conscious action.

If you're angry, ask yourself what you can do to transform that energy. Rage, frustration, disillusionment, grief, fear, despair – all of these emotions have the potential to be transmuted into something new. But first, they need to be properly felt. Passion is anger alchemized. Rise up. Stand up. Act up. Move your body. Rest long and deep. Transmute.

You don't need to want to save the planet to transform energy into a force for good. Use it whichever way you like. Don't stagnate and absorb. You may be called to protect. To speak out. To have your voice heard, or to be the voice of those who don't have one.

Or you may be called to create change in your own life. In your own body. In your constellation. In your mind. In your nervous system. In your cells. In your garden. It's in these times that the most beautiful and moving art is created. It's in these times that quantum leaps are made possible. It's in these times that we can cause a shift in the critical mass.

Let the times we're living in move you into action. It doesn't matter which action you choose. Whether you protest, paint, love, or activate. Whether you write, declutter, dance, or speak. Whether you run, swim, petition, protest or support, sing, or create – all that matters is that you do something. That you use this energy, this fear, this aggression, this sadness, this privilege, this complacency. Use it all.

The nervous system of the planet is recalibrating. And at the same time ours is too. We're the creators of this new world. We're the future human. We're in the crucible of the fire. We can use the heat. We can transmute it into something helpful. Together we can and are birthing a new human age.

SOUL INQUIRY

What emotions do you feel in your body?

How are you being called to use or transform that energy?

What is the Earth calling you to do?

△
TOOLS TO SEED THE LIGHT AND PLANT YOURSELF HERE

We are children of the stars and the Earth. The stars are constantly showering emanations onto the crystalline grid of the Earth. The Earth also sends information back up to the stars. Many Starseeds have come to the Earth to activate the ancient codes of wisdom that humanity's forgotten; and all of that information is stored in the crystalline grid.

The following meditations are my favorite ways to seed the light of your soul and plant yourself here. They'll allow you to be the bridge between the heavens and the Earth that's so needed at this time. They're grounded in nature and connect you to the universal forces of the Earth and the cosmos. Trust which meditations you're called toward.

You can record yourself reading the meditations out loud, or if you prefer, you can find recorded versions available at www. letterstoastarseed.com.

△
EARTH PULSING

There's a mysterious pulse woven through all of Life. The planet itself has a rhythm: You can see it in the seasons and the tides. Earth itself is connected with the same pulse that causes the planets to spin. In our modern world of artificial lighting, long work hours, conveniences, and free will, it's easy for us to get stuck and feel off-kilter.

Earth Pulsing is my favorite tool for surrendering to the pulse of not only the planet but the entire Universe, for the planet is part of this incredible, immeasurable Universe in which we live. I first created this practice as a way of surrendering to the feminine – a way to move from my own personal will to that of the Great Mother herself. It's a powerful tool for rejuvenation, surrender, cellular healing, and being held in the arms of the Earth. It's incredibly simple and unexpectedly powerful.

HOW TO DO THE EARTH PULSING PRACTICE

Lie down with your back to the Earth (if you can't get out into nature to do this, you can lie on the floor and imagine that you're lying on the Earth).

Draw your attention to your heart space, particularly focusing on the back of your heart, which is connected to the ground beneath you. Imagine your beautiful soul flower opening as you breathe in deeply. Slow down your breath so that you're breathing into all corners of your belly and invite the oxygen to travel into and nourish every cell in your body.

*Tune in to the pulse of your heart. Allow your own pulse
to slow down. To calm down. Begin to feel the pulse at the
back of your heart pulsing against the Earth beneath you.*

*Tune in to the pulse of the Earth. The pulse of the Mother.
The pulse that's connected to all things in Life. Feel the
Great Mother and the Grandmothers holding you and
calling you back home to your natural rhythm. Breathing
very deeply, invite your own pulse to slow down and sync
with the natural rhythm of the planet, the Great Mother.
Allow your heartbeat to surrender to this mysterious rhythm
that's woven through all of Life. Surrender to that. Let your
heart beat in harmony with the pulse of the Earth, the Great
Mother, and all of Life. Take one final breath in reverence
and thanks to this mysterious pulse of Life.*

△
PILLAR OF LIGHT MEDITATION

Nothing is more powerful than light. Proper light is fierce, not fluffy, and nothing can penetrate it. If we open ourselves up to light, we can be a conduit for it, from the unlimited supply of Source in the heavens above and the Earth below our feet.

The Pillar of Light is a meditation that I do often. Some days I do it as my main meditation, but I also do a quick charge-up version several times a day without fail while I'm washing the dishes, sitting at my desk, or walking down the street.

You can do the meditation at any time – while making dinner or as a sitting or standing meditation. You can do it when you're scared or when you feel as if you'd like some protection. It connects you to the Life force itself. It strengthens your energetic field and connects you to the fierce power of light above and below, with you as the bridge between the two. As above, so below.

Practicing the Pillar of Light meditation will strengthen your energetic system, soothe your nervous system, activate your light body, connect you with the wisdom of the Earth and the heavens above, seed your soul into your body more fully, and open you up to new levels of receiving and universal flow. It'll also assist in the anchoring of heaven on Earth (as above, so below).

The more you practice the meditation the thicker the pillar of light will get. The idea is that eventually the pillar will become wider than your physical body. However, just as with anything, we have to work at it, so at first it might appear to be thinner than your spine.

HOW TO DO THE PILLAR OF LIGHT MEDITATION

Slow down your breathing – breathe in and out very deeply and into all corners of your belly. Close your eyes if that feels good. As you're breathing, imagine really drinking in whatever it is that you need right now.

Imagine a ball of light in the heavens above. This is the unlimited supply of Source energy and it never runs out. Imagine a pillar/channel of this pure clear light energy coming down from the heavens.

Open the crown chakra at the top of your head to receive this powerful pillar of light from Source as it travels through the center of your body. Draw it from the crown of your head through your entire system, right down to the root chakra at the base of your spine, and down your legs. Let it travel through the Earth beneath you, through all of the layers of the Earth, until it hits a luminous blue crystal at the core of the planet. Imagine the pure cosmic light source of the Universe/heavens flowing on through.

Now allow yourself to receive another pillar/channel of light – this time, from the crystal in the center of the Earth itself. Allow it to travel through the layers of the Earth, through the crust of the planet, up your legs, through your system, past your heart center, out of the crown of your head and up to the unlimited ball of Source energy above.

Continue receiving this pillar of pure light source energy from above and below – allowing an exchange from the heavens and the cosmic Earth. As the pillar of light gets thicker and thicker imagine it charging you up and creating a field of protection, knowing that nothing can penetrate light. The thicker the pillar of light gets, the more protected and recharged you become. Continue receiving this pillar of light from above and below as you receive the intelligent light from the heavens and the intelligent light from the ancient Earth. Breathe deeply, knowing you're anchoring heaven on Earth as you do so.

△
STAR BATHING MEDITATION

This is a really beautiful meditation that connects you with the cosmos. When people star bathe they can experience a feeling of expansiveness and wonder, as well as the potential of receiving intelligence and downloads from the stars themselves. If you resonate with being a Starseed soul then you can also open yourself up to connecting with the star systems to which you feel most connected, to receive energetic downloads or rememberings. When opening yourself up to this, always open sacred soul space (see the chapter 'The Akashic Records' on page 40) to set a held container first.

Most of us resonate with the feeling of 'awe' we get when we take time to observe the stars at night. Star bathing takes this a step further, allowing the energy from the night sky to enter our personal energetic field so we can swim in the power and possibility of the great unknown. Doing so can give us a sense of perspective as we connect with something greater than ourselves or any issue or problem in this world. Studies have shown that the feeling of awe can lead to an increase in generosity and happiness, and enhance our ability to make decisions.

Star bathing is also great for creativity and intuition. As you take the time to star bathe, your right brain (which is responsible for creative and intuitive thinking) is activated. I believe that there are creations and consciousness waiting to be birthed onto the planet right now. So, if you're a creative, an entrepreneur, or any kind of inventor, then you could choose to dedicate your star bathing to receiving the inspiration and ideas that are wanting to be birthed through you at this time. It's also just beautiful to receive the healing, calming energy that the stars wish to shower us in!

HOW TO DO THE STAR BATHING MEDITATION

To begin, lie down on the Earth, on the floor, or on a bed, and close your eyes. Get yourself really comfortable and in complete receiving mode.

Release any tension that your body's holding by breathing in really deeply and holding your breath for five seconds. Release and exhale, letting go of anything your body is holding on to. Breathing deeply and freely, allow yourself to surrender completely and prepare to receive.

Visualize yourself on a tropical island. The air around you is warm and pleasant and you're lying on lush, juicy, green grass. The Earth beneath you is activated and pulsating with life.

Allow yourself to focus on one particular star, or on one particular cluster of stars, and allow yourself to be drawn to them. Breathe and receive the starlight streaming down from above you.

Allow yourself to receive the emanations of this starlight, showering into the very center of your heart and every single cell of your body. Notice how powerful this cosmic shower feels – so powerful and so gentle, all at once.

As the stars shower you with their light, open yourself up to receiving even more of your cosmic nature. Receive even more of your own star nature, and even more memory of your cosmic self, your star self, of the origins of your own soul.

Slowly begin to bring your attention back to the room, moving your fingers and toes. Gently open your eyes and come back to the here and now, feeling deeply replenished and fully alive.

Δ

LIGHT CODES MEDITATION

The third activation meditation is the Light Codes meditation. Here we'll be connecting with the power and energetic frequency of the Sun. You can do this meditation outdoors in the sunshine if it's not too hot. Imagine feeling the beautiful emanations of the Sun's rays when you do this meditation.

This is a cellular upgrade meditation in which you're really receiving the codes of light from the Sun. I believe there's a universal link between receiving light codes from the Sun and creating changes at a cellular level. Consciously absorbing the Sun's rays (in a sensible way to avoid sunburn) can bring long-term benefits as our DNA is activated by the light codes – leading to increased consciousness and spiritual awareness.

HOW TO DO THE LIGHT CODES MEDITATION

To begin, lie down on the Earth, on the floor, or on a bed. Or, if you find it more comfortable, you're welcome to sit on a chair, or on the Earth itself, with your spine completely straight.

Begin to close your eyes, and open yourself up to receiving the light, and the codes within the light, of the Sun. Breathe, and feel the Sun's rays traveling down to your face and your body.

Breathe, and imagine the Sun's rays carrying codes of light. Codes with information to upgrade your cells. Codes that carry information to upgrade your DNA. Codes that carry the deepest of healing. Codes that carry what you yearn for most. Breathe and receive these codes of light.

Be completely charged up by the energy of the Sun. Breathe, and be recharged, reignited, and reborn. Receive the light codes from the Sun.

When you're ready, take a deep breath in and stretch your body in whatever way feels good. Move your fingers and toes. Begin to open your eyes and prepare to go about your day, replenished and recharged.

△

SWEET HEALING WATERS MEDITATION

In this practice we're tapping into the sweet, sweet waters of Mother Earth herself. Those sweet healing waters that fill the sacred wells all around the world. We're also tapping into the memory of the time before we incarnated, when we were in between the worlds – in the water world of the Mother's womb where all of our needs were met and we remembered why we'd chosen to come.

This is such a calming, soothing activation meditation, one that'll bring deep replenishment; it's great to turn to it when you're feeling a bit empty, parched, or in need of healing.

HOW TO DO THE SWEET HEALING WATERS MEDITATION

Find somewhere you can get really comfortable. If you can, I recommend lying down on the Earth, on the floor, or even on a bed. If you feel called, you can also do this meditation while lying in a warm bath. Begin to close your eyes and invite your body and every single cell to enter a state of relaxation. Breathe in and out very deeply, and allow every part of you to be soothed, opening yourself up to a state of deep, deep healing.

Imagine yourself standing in front of the most beautiful natural springs you've ever seen. Nature's healing waters. Nature's healing bath. The waters of the Great Mother

Earth. You begin very safely making your way into the waters and start to float on your back. The warm water effortlessly cradles and holds you.

Begin drinking in whatever minerals and water and replenishment you need.

Breathe, and allow yourself to be weightless. Breathe, and allow yourself and your body to drink in whatever it is that you need right now. Allow yourself to breathe in the healing waters of this beautiful natural spring.

Breathe, and receive the rejuvenation. Let every part of your body and your mind and your soul be soothed. Breathe, and be weightless. Breathe, and surrender. Breathe, and drink it all in. Breathe, and be healed.

Allow yourself to drink in these healing waters, which are connected to the most sacred waters on the planet. Breathe, and drink in the healing. Breathe, and be healed. Breathe, and quench whatever deep thirst your body, mind, or soul has right now. Breathe, and drink in the healing waters. Breathe, and just float. Breathe, and be healed. Breathe, and return to your wholeness. Breathe, and remember why you chose to come.

Take a deep breath in, and begin to make your way out of the natural spring bath. Dry yourself off with a beautiful towel.

Feeling completely replenished and wholly healed, begin to bring yourself back to the here and now, and open your eyes.

Δ

THE GREAT CONSTELLATION

The Celtic word *Imrama* means a journey of the soul – a voyage on which we don't know where we're going but our soul knows the way. Many Starseeds resonate with the experience of being led to physical places on the Earth. For some this might be in the form of a trip, while for others, it may be physically moving there; and where travel isn't possible, it could be through connecting in some other, non-physical, way.

These places could be sacred sites, energetically powerful places on the planet, or places of our ancestry. The ancients knew about the power places of the planet, and many cultures, including the Aztecs and the Maya in Central America and the ancient Egyptians, built temples and places of worship in perfect alignment with the stars. You'll find more details about this in the chapter 'Reaching Back to the Ancients' on page 14.

Ley lines are invisible pathways on the land along which energy travels. They can be sensed when we tune in to them with our subtle senses. Also known as spirit paths, ley lines have been compared to the meridian system of the body used in Chinese medicine, and they link sacred sites, stone circles, burial mounds, and places of worship worldwide.

I live and work on the Mary ley line in Somerset, England, and on my morning walk I go to where the Mary and Michael ley lines meet. For many years I was led (most often spontaneously) to the land where I now live. At the time I didn't have children and I ran my own business, so it was easy for me to follow the call and do my work while on the move.

In Australian Aboriginal culture, songlines were the paths traveled by the creator beings as they made the land and sea during the Dreaming. These paths were recorded in the traditional songs and dances of the people, allowing them to access information about the land's history and to travel safely across great distances.

When we journey to places that our soul remembers, a shift takes place – both within us and on the planet. Ancient codes from long ago are activated within our cells, our soul, and the Earth itself. Or we are called to cross the country, climb a mountain, lie on the desert floor, or drink from an ancient well.

Are you being called to travel to a sacred place that your soul remembers? Or to tend the land on which you live? To honor and acknowledge the known and unknown keepers, custodians, or spirits of that land? As you connect with the Earth and honor its keepers, the land opens up more fully to hold you; the fruits provide more nourishment, and the guardians watch over you.

If you're called to visit a place that your soul remembers and it's different from your ancestral lineage, it's always important to be mindful and give back. Show reverence for the people and cultures that have been guardians of these places and give generously in return.

When we visit sacred sites, we can tap into the ancient wisdom of this time. Often, seeds of light are woken up in us and also in the Earth, and this is part of the concept of seeding the light.

Ancient myths allude to the existence of lost lands of the Earth, beyond what our documented history suggests. Some think that these lost lands exist in the past, while others believe they exist still today on a different dimension. As always, I encourage you to do your own research, to tune in and decide for yourself.

There's a crystalline grid within the Earth. It sings ancient and wise. The energies of the stars shower down on it and it sends information back. Starseeds are called to places on the grid. To anchor and seed, to protect and guard. When you visit a place you're called to, something is unlocked within it and something is unlocked within you too.

STARSEED ACTIVATION

'I honor, acknowledge, and thank the Keepers of the Earth beneath me and around me, known and unknown.

I open myself up to activating, unlocking, and receiving the wisdom of the Earth beneath me.

Thank you, thank you, thank you.

Please guide me, please lead me, please show me the way.'

△
WE ARE SEPARATE TOGETHER

I read the other day that the more ancient the soul, the deeper the soul's cave. Perhaps this is true. Many people who identify with being a Starseed often enjoy their own company. Spending time alone can be comforting, and at times necessary.

I know I needed that as a young girl – when the family were all together I'd go to my room and close the door. I didn't know it at the time, but that was my way of dealing with being with so many people all day at school and standing on the bus for an hour to and from school. My room was my refuge. It was where I could recharge, empty, and hear my soul speak.

This continued when I started working and once again had to commute. Like so many, I'd ride a packed train each day, crammed in like a sardine. Like many, I needed alone time to recalibrate. Today, as a mother, I'm not able to find the same amount of time in my day to be alone; it comes in smaller windows but still, I benefit from it when I can. It helps to know this about myself so I can do my best to get these needs met.

Many find it more nourishing to retreat than to spend their time in meaningless or unaligned conversations and relationships. Now that my life is more aligned – or I know who I am so I know how to align my life to that – I don't need as much time away from it. But I still find I need to go into my cave any time I've gone out into the world, for example, to teach a workshop or film a course. Tide goes in, tide goes out. If you have a friend who's a single mum or dad and has no choice but to be always on, perhaps the greatest gift you could give them would be the gift of a little bit of time to replenish their energy.

While it's normal to need to take refuge to replenish our reserves, we must also remember that we're not here to go about this life alone. Humans are pack animals and we all need the love, company, and support of others – both emotionally and physically. If you have a friend who's living alone, perhaps the greatest gift you could give them is holding a hug a little longer than normal.

In our increasingly online world, we can be 'connected' to more people than ever yet feel more alone and isolated than ever. There's still so much we don't know about the energetic side effects of things like social media, with so many people knowing our 'news.' What's it doing to our auric field? There's no connection that beats physical connection, except when that physical connection comes from someone who truly sees the ancient soul present within.

SOUL INQUIRY

How can you reach out physically to people in your life?

△
ACKNOWLEDGING OUR OTHERNESS AS A PATH TO ONENESS

Sometimes, acknowledging otherness is a necessary path to true, sustainable oneness. As souls we intrinsically remember unity and thus it's natural to yearn for it here on Earth. Perhaps this is why it feels so painful when we experience the opposite. But it's crucial to remember that we can't simply overlook reality and pretend that unity, love, and forgiveness are here. This is one of the greatest challenges for Starseeds.

To bring about authentic unity we must first acknowledge the ways in which both we and the world have been divisive (personally, ancestrally, and collectively): The shadows, hate, wounds, separation, severing, wrongs, and sadness. And no one is immune to this work.

It seems that in these changing times we're being called to go back in order to leap forward. To ride the pendulum as it swings and gathers us all into alignment. We're learning that it's crucial for us to acknowledge what's been severed and how we've been divided and dividing (our otherness) in order to find our way back to each other (our oneness).

I believe that we're each being called to hold the vision for genuine unity, and at the same time, reweave the sacred thread of humanity that's been severed, through guided, grounded action.

We're living in divisive times. When we're hurt and triggered we tend to see things as a personal attack rather than as an opportunity for healing. If we're to find true peace and unity, we need to drop our defenses and see things as Rumi suggested – outside of right and wrong. To dive both high and deep and remember that we all came here to work through this and we're all part of the one human family.

Many of us who chose to be here right now are being called to explore how we, our ancestors, and society have, consciously and unconsciously, inflicted pain on others. How the systems that we learn from and live in need to crumble in order to be rebuilt. How true oneness isn't possible until all are treated as precious, sacred, and holy.

Many of us who chose to be here right now are being invited to gather the courage to drop the armor and see things as they truly are for all people. To say 'I'm sorry' with an open heart and mean it. To be part of the healing rather than the perpetuation of inherited conflict or oppression. To play our part, in our own small way, in healing our ancestral lines through our own healing. This isn't about blame or shame or getting to some static healed state – it's about unwinding the patterning that got us here and opening our hearts to ourselves, the Earth, and each other. Acknowledging that we're here. And here we are.

SOUL INQUIRY

How are you being called to drop your defenses and unwind past wrongs? What are you sorry for?

△
YOU CAN'T BUY DEVOTION

Leading in ordinary times is challenging enough, but leading in times of change is a whole other thing. Since you're reading this, you're likely being called to be a leader in times of change. And these are certainly changing times.

It's impossible to lead in a sustainable way without being led from within. And so the best advice is always to be led from within. When we lead from within we're choosing to tune in to the wisdom of our soul and take action on that. To listen to our inner voice over any external input. To trust the intelligence that's seeded within us and available to us every moment of every day.

The best way to be led from within is to develop a regular practice of going within – to develop a devotional practice with the deepest of roots. The more you show up, the clearer the voice gets and the deeper the roots become. The clearer the voice gets, the easier it is to trust. The deeper the roots become, the more unshaken by external opinions, judgments, projections, and pressures you become.

The devotional practice will vary from person to person and it may change significantly over time. The more you show up to be led from within, the easier leading will become. Commit to being soul-led. The more you step forth on your soul's path, the more external input, projections, and pressure from the outside world you'll likely get. The external world will always want something from you, and the more people who look to you to lead them, the more differing opinions and projections you'll have coming your way.

As a leader you'll likely be asked to do many things that could take you down many different paths. These could be the best opportunities in the world; however, if a path's not in alignment with your soul's path it's not the path for you.

The more visible you become, the more important it is to turn your gaze within. The more important it is to be vigilant about staying on and deeply knowing your own inner path. To showing up without waver; and to always, always being led from the seeds planted deep within.

You can't buy devotion. It can only be gathered by showing up day after day after day. Perhaps it's carried over from lifetime to lifetime too.

As a leader in this new era your devotion is what will be felt. And your discernment is what will be valued.

People will be able to sense if you're in it merely for personal or external gain. It'll be felt if you're being influenced by the external hecklers, or if you're in it for them, for we, for thee. Play the long game for all of humanity. Put your devotion first.

When we show up to our devotional practice and develop this relationship of being inwardly led, we find it easier to know and trust our path. We attract that which is truly for us and we're able to discern what's not. It's easier to stay in alignment with who we are as a soul. That which is meant for us starts moving toward us like a magnet, and we no longer need to strive and push so much. We switch from my will to thy will. We go from trying to control and manipulate, and strive and shift, into deep, true surrender.

In order to live a life of devotion, a devotional practice is imperative. Whether that's meditation, chanting, prayer, or something else, it doesn't matter – all that matters is that we're forever tending and sourcing from within. The more you show up to your devotional practice the more you'll be held. The more you're held, the easier the devotion becomes. You are carried. You're not doing it for an outcome, but rather your whole life becomes one big, moving prayer.

SOUL INQUIRY

What does your existing devotional practice look like?

Are you being called to show up in a different way or with more consistency?

△

For Those Going through Sacred Pain

Soon, these times of sacred rebirthing will be over.
Soon. Soon. Soon.
These moments of devastating
s e p a r a t i o n,
of polarity,
of being misunderstood, of confusion, of not being seen or heard...
And while just now we may not be able to see the end
in sight, from the perspective of the soul what we are
in is but a breath in the timeline of the Earth.

This moment matters. You came here for this. We all have
our own personal syllabus. And some day, some decade or
century soon, what feels like it will matter, will not.

So trust your part in the sacred play. Trust that these times
are birthing times for the future of humanity. For all of us —
both individually and collectively. Holy rebirthing times.

The one must fall for true Oneness to reign. It's both about
you and not about you. Trust your part in the sacred labor.
In the contractions. In the pressure. In the darkness. In the p u s h.

In the void we will birth ourselves
and discover that what we thought was a tomb is actually a womb.
After winter sweetness will return once more.
It is the law of the Earth.

△

THE CHILDREN OF THE SUN ARE COMING

The Children of the Sun are coming. They're so very near. In fact, some are already here. It's our job to pave the way for them. To keep the light behind their eyes beaming bright. To never let it disappear. Some of these souls haven't been here before, but we've been with them. Do you remember? They're ready to be here now. Some are already here.

There are souls coming that the mystics have been calling the golden ones. They come in knowing, remembering, present, clear. We must do what we can now to clear the way for them – to chisel the container within ourselves for their arrival. To prepare the garden, to open the borders, to destroy the walls, to abolish the separation, to open the gates, **to return to the arms of the Earth**. For them and for us.

Sensitive and strong. Awake and intelligent. Soul woven into matter. The great Grandmothers have been weaving for and dreaming of their arrival. They're so almost here.

We must do what we can to preserve their innocence by remembering our own. By growing up, by being reborn while still fully living. By finding a way to become more and more alive as we age, by incarnating more and more fully. To open, open, open.

They're lining up to come: To be birthed, welcomed, and recognized by those who have refused to stay asleep. They're calling forth the guardians of the Earth. The future ancestors. The elders of the Earth.

The Great Reunion

There will come a time when the souls
of the unknown meet the family of humanity.
When we'll no longer relive the agony of separation
through erecting borders, fences, and walls.
When we'll realize that each one of us is made of the
same ancient starstuff in body, mind, bone, and soul.
The earth and the cosmos breathing itself in and out,
in and out since the beginning of the circling of time.
When we'll find our way back to each other,
for our survival depends on each other.
When we'll embrace our differences and our similarities.
When we'll know that change isn't only inevitable but our most natural state.
When we'll be reunited with our brothers
and sisters of planets and stars familiar.
When hearts will be wide and communication will be free.
When home will be everywhere. everywhere. everywhere. ev-
ywhere. everywhere. everywhere. everywhere. everywhere. everywhere. everywhere. ev-
ywhere. everywhere. everywhere. everywhere. everywhere. everywhere. everywhere. ev-

When we will cast a circle of love around all of humanity

That day is coming, that day is near, that day is coming.
May it be almost here.

Δ

Ascend to the Earth

The answers for us right now are not elsewhere in the stars.
They're not in the heavens either.
They're right here, on Earth, in the seed in the soil.

Everything we seek is waiting for us here.
On Earth as it is in heaven.
Don't you remember that you are the seed?
Don't you remember why you chose to come?

Find the holy seeded within every tree, every stone,
every animal, every human, every heart, every cell.
Precious, precious child of star and Earth.
Soul experiencing itself for a breath.
Star seeded for just a moment in matter.

You went through a lot to be here at this time.
Won't you be here now?

Be like the flower.
Seed and bloom without caring what others think.
And when it's time, and you will know when,
Throw your petals to the wind
For the chance to do it over and over again.
Remember why you have come.

Ascend to the Earth.

△
ACKNOWLEDGMENTS

To the team at Hay House UK, especially Michelle Pilley, who asked me to write this book while also honoring my timing until my answer was a guided 'yes.' Thank you for your wisdom, guidance, and support. To Debra Wolter, Julie Oughton, Leanne Siu Anastasi, and Jo Burgess, thank you for your attention to detail, skill, and support in creating this book with such dedication, kindness, and compassion.

To Amy Kiberd, my colleague, friend, and commissioning editor, with whom I shared the first seeds of this book many years ago. Working on this book with you was an unexpected blessing. Your presence in my life is a true gift and a constant encouragement. I appreciate and feel your support and know that my work is able to reach further because of it.

To Craig Gourlay, thank you for always encouraging me to take a higher viewpoint. You're a pillar in my life, allowing me to focus on what I came here to do. Your dedication, professionalism, devotion, and capacity inspire me again and again.

To Jade Perez, thank you for your devotion, dedication, professionalism, and presence. You keep the show on the road and do so with such grace and joy. I'm so grateful for your grounded work and support, and your holding of the Rise Sister Rise Membership is deeply felt.

To Rhiannon and Paula, thank you for your grounded, practical support in this year of all years. You're a blessing in our lives and have made it possible for this book to be in the world now.

To Binnie Dansby, thank you for your friendship, wisdom, witnessing, and encouragement for this book. You're a true gift in my life. Our friendship is one of my life's blessings.

To Robert Holden, thank you for your constant gentle steering, encouragement, and friendship. To Hollie Holden, thank you for being my whale sister and dearest friend – life wouldn't be the same without you and our walk and talks.

To Marion Ross, PhD and Tracy Latz, M.D., M.S., for our conversations on all things Starseed.

To Kyle Gray, thank you for walking this path with me, for your confidence, the daily calls, the trips, and the coffees. I think I might have written you into my contract for doing this work. You make it so much more fun.

To all of my teachers, some of whom I've known personally, and others whose work has moved and inspired me. To Sonia Choquette, who guided me through my twenties to trust my intuition and align my life to my spirit. To Andrrea Hess, creator of the Soul Realignment Course, which is one of the places I learned how to work with the Akashic Records in a structured way. To Alen Bock, who received information that underpins a lot of the material that entered my life early on in my journey. To Marion Woodman and Ram Das, whose work meets me in ways that I cannot quite express. To the thousands of people who worked with me when I was doing soul readings and soul blueprints, and all who have attended my workshops.

To Sheila Dickson, who is one of my oldest soul friends and the first person I called when I began reading about the concept of Starseeds. Your unwavering presence in my life from such a young age was so important for the work I do now. I'm so grateful I walked up those stairs more than 20 years ago. Thank you for seeing and understanding me.

To Madeline Giles, Eliza Reynolds, Amy Firth, Ahlea Khadro, Lou Androlia, Meggan Watterson, and Lisa Lister for your friendship, understanding, and presence. To Julia Dvinskaya and Sophie Knock for your conscious grounded support and expertise through the writing of this book.

To the Grandmothers of the Earth and the Council of Light, who were present while I was writing these pages. To the spirits of the land here in Glastonbury and the Chalice Well Guardians where a lot of this book was written. To all mystics who came before me and have made it possible for me to share my voice and work so freely.

To Sunny, thank you for choosing to come and planting me even more deeply than before. You've taught me more than anyone else and you're not even one yet! This book is for you.

△
REFERENCES

Ancient Stars in Our Bones

1. Schrijver, K. and Schrijver, I. (2015), *Living with the Stars: How the Human Body is Connected to the Life Cycles of the Earth, the Planets, and the Stars*, Oxford: Oxford University Press, p.1.

Reaching Back to the Ancients

1. Bhathal, R. (2006), 'Astronomy in Aboriginal culture': https://academic.oup.com/astrogeo/article/47/5/5.27/231805 [Accessed 3 September 2020]

2. Schorer, C.E. (1962), 'Indian Tales of C. C. Trowbridge: "The Star Woman"': www.jstor.com/stable/4317945 [Accessed 2 September 2020]

3. Bird, Grinnell, G. (1893), 'Pawnee Mythology': www.jstor.com/stable/533298 [Accessed 2 September 2020]

The Akashic Records

1. Todeschi, K. (2003), *Edgar Cayce on the Akashic Records*, Virginia Beach: A.R.E. Press.

BIBLIOGRAPHY

Barrett, Lisa Feldman (2017), *How Emotions Are Made*, USA: Pan Macmillan

Carey, Ken (1991), *The Starseed Transmissions*, New York: Harper Collins Publishers

Hess, Andrea (2010), *Soul Realignment Practitioner Training Level 1 & 2*

Leary, Dr. Timothy (1973), *Starseed*, San Francisco: Level Press

Leeming, David and Margaret (1994), *A Dictionary of Creation Myths*, New York: Oxford University Press

MacLead, Sharon Paice (2018), *Celtic Cosmology and the Otherworld*, North Carolina: McFarland & Company Inc. Publishers

Marciniak, Barbara (1948), *Earth*, Vermont: Bear & Company Inc

Marciniak, Barbara (1992), *Bringers of the Dawn*, Vermont: Inner Traditions/Bear & Company

Melchizedek, Drunvalo (2000), *The Ancient Secret of the Flower of Life*, Volumes 1 & 2, Arizona: Light Technology Publishing

Shier, Susan Taylor (2014), *Soul Mastery*, Colorado: Velvet Springs Press

Sproul, Barbara (1991), *Primal Myths*, New York: Harper One

Steiger, Brad (1976), *Gods of Aquarius*, USA: Harcourt Brace Jovanvich

Temple, Robert (1976), *The Sirius Mystery*, USA: St Martin's Press

Wilkinson, Philip (2009), *Myths & Legends*, London: Penguin Random House

△
GOING DEEPER

If you'd like to continue exploring Rebecca's work or the themes in this book, the following resources will support you.

Letters to a Starseed website

Discover meditations, the book playlist, and other tools mentioned in the book at www.letterstoastarseed.com

Rise Sister Rise membership

The best way to work with Rebecca is to join her Membership; www.rebeccacampbell.me/membership

Discover Your Cosmic Blueprint online course

Unlock your soul's unique history in this powerful online course; www.rebeccacampbell.me/discoveryourcosmicblueprint

You Are The Oracle online course

The You Are The Oracle course guides you to connect with your inner oracle; www.rebeccacampbell.me/oracle

Newsletter

Receive notes, inspiration, and updates from Rebecca every fortnight; www.rebeccacampbell.me/newsletter

△
ALSO BY THE AUTHOR

The Starseed Oracle

Connect with the portal to your heart, remember who you are at a soul level, and unlock your soul's gifts; www.starseedoracle.me

Rise Sister Rise

A guide to unleashing the wise, wild woman within; www.risesisterrise.com

Light Is the New Black

A guide to answering your soul's calling and working your light; www.lightisthenewblack.com

The Work Your Light Oracle

Unlock your intuition, act on the calls of your soul, and live a life that's in alignment with the help of this beautiful, activated oracle; www.rebeccacampbell.me/oracledeck

△

ABOUT THE AUTHOR

Rebecca Campbell is a writer, mystic, visionary, philosopher, creative, and mother currently living in Glastonbury, England. Originally from the sunny shores of Sydney, Australia, as a young child Rebecca displayed a unique fascination with the journey of the soul, the mysteries, and the inner life.

She experienced her first awakening as a young teenager and has been studying the intuitive mystic arts ever since. At the age of 18 Rebecca answered an inner call to go on a solo pilgrimage to initiate herself in the sacred sites of the UK and Ireland, the countries where she has spent the majority of her adult life.

She has published several best-selling books and oracle decks and teaches both internationally and virtually. Her work supports people to remember that they are nature and to connect to the wisdom of their soul and live in alignment with that.

Rebecca's mission is to weave the soul back into everyday life. Her creations and the *Three Steps to Living a Soul-Led Life* have transformed the lives of hundreds of thousands of people all around the world.

 www.rebeccacampbell.me

 @rebeccacampbell_author

 @rebeccacampbellauthor

Newsletter: www.rebeccacampbell.me/newsletter

△
DO YOU WANT TO DISCOVER MORE ABOUT WHO YOU ARE AS A SOUL?

The *Discover Your Cosmic Blueprint* online course is a dynamic investigation into your own soul. In it, Rebecca will guide you with practical, powerful techniques to help you discover your cosmic roots, unearth your past lifetimes, and map your unique soul history.

This experiential online course, which can be studied at your own pace is available now. This course will help you to:

- Document your soul's journey by creating the book of your soul.

- Awaken to your higher purpose and step into who you came here to be.

- Develop your intuitive senses and learn to trust your inner guidance.

Discover more here:

www.rebeccacampbell.me/discoveryourcosmicblueprint

HAY HOUSE

Look within

Join the conversation about latest products,
events, exclusive offers and more.

f   Hay House

🐦   @HayHouseUK

📷   @hayhouseuk

🖤   healyourlife.com

We'd love to hear from you!